Invitations

All Bible references are from the New International Version unless otherwise indicated.

Word Association Publishers
205 Fifth Avenue
Tarentum, Pennsylvania 15084
www.wordassociation.com
1.800.827.7903

ISBN: 978-1-63385-232-7

Library of Congress Control Number: 2017918392

Invitations

A HANDBOOK FOR
INTERACTIVE WORSHIP
BEYOND THE ALTAR CALL

BY THE RT. REV. DOUGLAS BROOKS WEISS

DEDICATION

I see, hear, and experience Jesus in my wife, Eleanor, everyday. She speaks the truth in love, holding me accountable and steadfast to God's call and purposes. Her editorial gifts clarify my thoughts, making what I write readable. She is God's blessing and an expression of His amazing grace to me.

I'm deeply grateful to the staff and congregation at Christ the King Church who helped develop the scripts. Eloise Martindale, a woman of deep faith and intense creativity, helped research and construct the presentations. The worship that flowed from the scripts was shaped and undergirded by an anointed music team led by the Rev. Jeff Towle and his wife, Paula.

The insights and proof reading skills of the reading team were invaluable: Dale and Barbara Traven, Tom and Andie Hutton, Carolyn Lamberth, Lindsey Anderson Saler, and Bishop John Rodgers, Jr. After the input of the reading team was incorporated, Lisa Hawkins generously offered to edit the book. Her faith and wisdom yielded more of Jesus and less of me.

Most of all, my gratitude is to God's people at St. Mark's, Shelby, Ohio, and Christ the King Church, Campbell, California, who joined in the experiment of invitational interactive worship. They are my inspiration as royal and holy priests in the service of the Lord Jesus Christ.

CONTENTS

INTRODUCTION

INVITATIONS abounded in Jesus' ministry. Everywhere He went Jesus made invitations. Even though His invitations were usually welcoming and hospitable, they included the possibility for confrontation, conviction, confession, and forgiveness. He called people to repentance and to take up their cross and follow Him. Jesus invited people to hear a teaching, receive a blessing, have a need met, or share a meal. God's only begotten Son made invitations that drew people into a deeper relationship with Him and one another.

Today Jesus continues to invite us to come to Him with needs that demand our attention. We often carry heavy loads of responsibility that sap our strength and find us yearning for rest. In Jesus there is rest, refreshment, and strength. His invitations promise a future grounded in victory and filled with hope. Jesus' invitations are far more transformative than most invitations. They also turn the tables about who is in charge. We want to be in charge of our lives, but Jesus invites us to allow Him to take control. This is the foundational invitation.

Jesus invites us to receive salvation and new life through Him. The apostle John's words are unequivocal and bold. *"For God so loved the world that he gave his one and only Son, that whoever believes in him shall not perish but have eternal life. For God did not send his Son into the world to condemn the world, but to save the world through him. Whoever believes in him is not condemned, but whoever does not believe stands condemned already because they have not believed in the name of God's one and only Son."* [1]

In today's church the "altar call" is the remnant of Jesus' foundational invitation. Jesus invited people to put their faith in Him as their personal Savior and Lord. An altar call makes the same invitation. Of course, not everyone responds positively. I certainly didn't. I reacted negatively to my first experience of an altar call, which happened my first year in college. That reaction stayed with me for many years. I objected to the idea of an altar call because of the way it was done. It seemed manipulative. I imagine I am not alone in a knee-jerk negative reaction.

When I was a newly ordained Episcopal priest, my leadership of worship was devoid of invitations, even the foundational one. I allowed my clergy collar to form a barrier between the congregation and myself. I held God's people at arm's length. God eventually brought down my barriers, just as He crumbled the walls of Jericho.

Later in ministry, God and a few fellow pastors encouraged me to experiment with worship. In turn, I risked inviting my congregation to put their whole self – body, soul and spirit – into corporate worship. The results were astounding! We transitioned from simply gleaning information from Holy Scripture to applying that information to our lives. We grew in Christian character, embracing

---

1   John 3:16-18

our role as a royal priesthood of believers.[2] Concurrently, the parish grew in membership, ministry and mission.

What I will be presenting in this book is a different "worldview" of the worship service. Rather than a clergy driven event, I propose worship as an invitational and interactive experience that addresses the needs of people. In doing so, it equips believers and allows them to practice ministry in the church before going into the world. For this to happen, clergy must relinquish control of worship and listen to the Holy Spirit's promptings to issue invitations that connect people with God and one another. These invitations should be consistent with the order of worship, Bible readings, and sermon themes. Invitations in the context of worship address needs for healing in body, soul and spirit. They confront difficult situations, build relationships, foster godly character, and assist followers to become disciples and ambassadors of the Father's kingdom.

God has entrusted clergy with the responsibility of nurturing and equipping believers for ministry. Equipping believers means clergy give away what they have been given. Interactive invitational worship provides a process to do this. It encourages clergy to entrust ministries to believers according to their gifts and abilities. Why? Because the followers of Jesus Christ are *"a royal priesthood, a holy nation, God's special possession...."* [3] Jesus promised that believers would do the *"works I have*

---

2   Exodus 19:5-6 & 40:15; 1 Peter 2:5+9
3   1 Peter 2:9

been doing, and they will do even greater things...."[4] Clergy are called to serve and mentor people in the Church so that they can be and do all that God has purposed for them as individuals and as a Christian community. Often believers who accept invitations and receive the ministry of prayer become prayer ministers themselves. Throughout forty years of ministry, I've seen that interactive invitational worship can transform a church. I believe what God has shown me will enrich both clergy and worshipers. My fervent prayer is that everyone who reads this book will be blessed and challenged.

Included in the book are scripts for **The Ten Gates of Nehemiah's Jerusalem** and **The Tabernacle:** *God's Portrait of Jesus Christ.* They are the result of one congregation's experience of connecting the prophecies of the Messiah in the Old Testament with Jesus Christ's fulfillment of those prophecies in the New Testament. Coming to this understanding was a process, not an event. It took twenty years. The scripts welcome worshippers into God's presence, offering opportunities to engage with and respond to His Word, His presence, and His people.

First and foremost, the scripts are tools for clergy to practice making invitations and for congregations to respond to them. Their responses solidify commitments to the Lord while furthering the process of Christian maturity. The scripts also assist believers in identifying the spiritual gifts God has entrusted to them. Believers are equipped

---

4   John 14:12

for *"works of service, so that the body of Christ may be built up."* [5] The scripts are a way to begin establishing interactive invitational worship within the life of a congregation. The invitations, responses, and resulting ministry strengthen the church while glorifying God.

What has been given to me, I entrust to you. You are free to use the scripts in full or in part, alter them, and give them to others. Look to the Father. Listen to Jesus. Do what the Holy Spirit reveals to you.

---

5   Ephesians 4:12

FOUNDATIONAL INVITATIONS FOR ME

AT THE HEART of our relationship with God is the invitation to receive and follow Jesus Christ as our personal Savior and Lord. The Gospels are filled with accounts of Jesus making invitations, but somehow I missed the importance of this aspect of His ministry. It wasn't part of my education, either in seminary or in being mentored. I didn't understand the significance of Jesus' invitations until I experienced them myself.

Those invitational experiences planted the seed for a different type of worship. I did not come to the understanding and practice of invitational worship easily. It was a process involving God's revelation, the wise counsel of friends, and a number of fiery trials. I had to let go of my traditional understanding of a pastor's role to grasp what the Lord required of me. Ultimately, this meant relinquishing control of my life to Him and being attentive to His guidance.

I begin with the three invitations from the Lord that were foundational for me. Hopefully these stories will bless and encourage you, maybe even make you laugh.

Story: Shopping Center Revival

"You really have to see this! It'll blow your mind!" Rick was pressing me to attend a revival meeting that evening.

"Are you inviting me?"

"No, I went last night. It's wild, you won't believe it!" he insisted.

"I don't know," I said backing away.

"What's the big deal? You go to church all the time. Tonight's their last night. Go!"

"I'll think about it," I insincerely promised, turning to find a way out.

Later in the day, curiosity got the better of me, along with a twinge of what I would come to understand as conviction. It was the summer break after my freshman year at Lincoln College. My parents had moved from a large house in Rocky River, a western suburb of Cleveland, to a one-story bungalow in nearby Bay Village. Their relocation removed me from my limited circle of friends and took away my bedroom, sending a clear message, "Time to leave the nest. No turning back."

That I was actually *in* college was a miracle. I hadn't a clue where it was leading, so I stuck with my answer to the childhood question, "What do you want to be when you grow up?"

"A garbage man or a priest," was my stock answer that initially startled, then elicited laughter from questioners. College hadn't yet changed my answer, just the order of the options. Only later did I realize that both professions deal with the same thing - disposing of garbage.

With nothing better to do and nobody to hang out with, curiosity overcame fear. I found myself seated on a folding chair in the very last row of a vacant store in Bay Village's one and only shopping center. Although I'd been in church all my life, not one thing was familiar that entire evening.

A handful of enthusiastic choir members accompanied by an upright piano led a loud, frequently rambunctious congregation in unfamiliar, but accessible hymns. Involuntarily, I found myself singing.

The preacher was animated to an intensity that drew sweat from his brow. It dripped from his forehead into his eyes. I was put off by what I deemed to be his overly dramatic and manipulative delivery. In spite of his dramatics, I was captivated by what he was saying and doing. He wiped away the sweat with a hand towel, all the while shouting about the BIBLE! SINNERS! and JESUSSS! The beads of moisture on the preacher's forehead were matched by the perspiration that soaked my armpits. I wrestled with running out a nearby door or holding my ground. At one point, I found myself laughing, but with hot tears of guilt on my cheeks.

The preacher's voice softened to almost a whisper as he invited people, "Come forward and surrender your life to Jesus... right now... come on now... you know who you are. Jesus loves you. He wants to forgive you for ALL your SINS and welcome you home to be with HIM forever... come on now... HE'S INVITING YOU!" The preacher proclaimed God's invitation at full volume.

Somehow I resisted bolting through the door and escaping into the parking lot. All my life I'd known the Lord Jesus. My parents had offered me to Father God at my baptism as an infant. I'd faithfully served the Lord and His church as an acolyte since my sixth birthday. In my heart I knew He was calling me to more, but in that moment the Holy Spirit convicted me that I'd never truly given my life to Him. I made, not a step, but a halting stumble forward to where the preacher stood. Bible in hand, he led us in a prayer that we repeated after him word for word. I'd never done that before. The prayers I was familiar with were always read from a book and acknowledged with a reverent, "Amen."

Along with a handful of older people who had come forward, I vocally acknowledged to Jesus, "I'm a miserable sinner in need of saving." Together, phrase upon phrase, we thanked, "Jesus for forgiving me; for paying the debt of my sins, and the sins of the whole world." Then we prayed, "I give my life to You, Jesus… every bit of me to all of You. I ask You to be my personal Savior and Lord, right now, tonight." It didn't take but a moment to pray the prayer that ended with the entire congregation shouting, "Amen! Amen! Alleluia! Amen!"

Maybe it was the tears that blurred my sight, or the sense that I'd become disconnected from my body, but all I could think was, "I'm done. At least, I'll go to Heaven. Everything's OK." My legs gave out, and I crumpled to the floor. The man who helped me to my feet whispered in my ear, "It's the Holy Spirit, boy. Alleluia!"

I had no idea that I'd responded to an "altar call." I'd never heard of such a thing. That was Saturday night. Sunday morning I was in St. Barnabas Episcopal Church's sacristy, vesting to assist the parish priest at the 8:00 AM Holy Eucharist. Offhandedly, I mentioned that the previous night I had attended a revival meeting at the local shopping center. I was hoping to wedge an opening for a longer conversation. The priest's raised eyebrows and sober frown communicated his silent disapproval.

After the service, I drove to the shopping center and found that the rented chairs and the piano were gone. The storefront was once again entirely vacant. With no one to help me process my experience of the night before, I hid its mystery in my heart.

Story: A Conversation on Highway 71

After my ordination as a priest at the Church of the Epiphany in Euclid, Ohio, the Bishop moved Eleanor and me to St. Mark's, a struggling parish in the small town of Shelby. The pictures hanging outside the sacristy were of many senior wardens and some former clergy. The clergy photographs were of a few young men fresh from seminary and many more of priests nearing retirement. The photo gallery declared that this was a place of lay leadership where clergy began and ended ministry. I was another on the short list of beginners.

Four years into the pastorate at St. Mark's, I came to the end of myself. The congregation was thriving, but I was not. St. Mark's had grown from a failing parish to a vital congregation with creative programs and significant ecumenical community outreach. The ministry the Lord had entrusted to me was fruitful due to His grace and my hard work. In retrospect I realize that I was, and to some degree still am, a perfectionist and workaholic. Poor stewardship of those personal dynamics had depleted me. I was seriously considering other vocations. On the way to a diocesan meeting in Cleveland, God spoke to me audibly. "Douglas, I am aware of your exhaustion. I have heard you question My call upon your life. Surrender everything to Me. I want all of your life right now!"

I frantically checked the radio. It was off. "What's happening?" I whispered in fear. The voice was familiar. "I understand what You're asking of me, Lord," I said to the windshield, knowing that I had only offered Him those portions of my life I believed were acceptable – places where I had achieved a degree of competence. He was telling me to yield all of myself to Him immediately, particularly those areas that I had deluded myself into thinking He couldn't see. I had known and loved the Lord my entire life. This was the most difficult request that He had made of me. He was asking me to cease striving to put my life together solely by my own efforts. I pulled the car to the side of the freeway in tears.

"Lord, I've given You the bits and pieces of my life, my filthy rags of self-righteousness. There are places within me consumed in sin that I am helpless to address. I am truly a miserable sinner, and there is no health in me," I confessed. "I surrender all my life to You. I am ashamed of my sins. I repent and ask for Your forgiveness. Please cleanse and change me. I accept You again and more completely as my personal Savior and Lord." Quiet filled the car as the heaving sobs in my chest subsided. Time seemed suspended. Gradually I became aware of the car being rocked by the whoosh of passing traffic.

"Douglas, get back on the road or you'll be late for the meeting," He urged in a gentler, almost teasing tone.

"Yes, Sir." In that moment, I stopped searching for a way out of the ordained ministry.

PART I: FOUNDATIONAL INVITATIONS FOR ME

>☛ >☛ >☛

These two stories seem very different – separated by a decade, by denominations, by settings. Both the revival meeting and hearing God speak audibly may seem weird. But both stories demonstrate the centrality of an invitation. In both cases, God was repeatedly inviting me to continue in the process of becoming who He called me to be. He was inviting me to receive the fruit of His Spirit that defines Christian character and embraces His purpose for my life.

Story: Hospital Visit with Zorayda and Bob

Prayer isn't always when, where or with whom you expect. I was about to experience that truth as the new pastor of St. Mark's Episcopal Church. Standing watch following the Holy Eucharist, Zorayda scrutinized my every move to see that I not only removed my vestments properly, but also hung them in their prescribed locations on their designated hangers.

"One vestment per hanger, Father," she corrected.

"Sorry, I forgot."

"What will you do when I'm not here to keep an eye on you?"

"Toss the vestments over the back of a chair," I ventured.

"No doubt," she said with impatience. "No doubt. Men are so careless," she observed, cracking a smile.

"Zorayda, where's Bob this morning?" I asked, changing the subject. Her eyes lowered and somberness returned to her countenance. It appeared as though she was not going to answer.

"He's in the hospital," she finally responded in a shamed whisper.

"At Shelby Memorial?'

"No… in Columbus at Riverside."

"Zorayda, I'm so sorry to hear that. What happened? Is he going to be all right?" She looked away to hide the tears forming in her eyes.

"He's not well. I'm going to see him tomorrow. Would you come with me?"

"Of course."

Zorayda insisted on driving, choosing the comfort of her Cadillac over the economy of my Civic. The day was overcast. The climate in the car mirrored the weather outside. Zorayda said little. I honored her need for silence. We arrived at Riverside Hospital before noon. Zorayda ushered me to a secure area that required us to phone into a nurse's station. We identified ourselves and the patient we intended to visit. From my three years in Clinical Pastoral Education, I recognized that we were about to enter a psychiatric unit. My heart sank as the lock mechanism buzzed, releasing the bolt that allowed us to enter. The source of Zorayda's shame became clearer.

As I pulled the door open for Zorayda, chaotic noise burst through the opening, shattering the silence of the corridor in which we had waited. Inside, we headed for the nurse's station to check in and locate Bob. Patients wandered the hall aimlessly, in various states of disarray and undress. Their eyes were fixed in a chemically induced blank gaze. Many licked their lips and wiped their mouths as if this act would produce the moisture medications had stolen from their bodies. Conversations unfolded in spastic slow motion, like a child fiddling with the volume control of patients' lives.

Beside the nurses' desk, a man in mismatched pajamas and furry pink slippers with bunny ears was rummaging through a combination ashtray and trash receptacle. His back was to us as he pushed the sand around with his fingers looking for cigarette butts, all the while mumbling to himself, "Don't leave nothing for nobody. Gotta smoke… gotta smoke… yes… yes… gotta smoke." He pulled a butt from the sand and, with trembling hands, struggled to straighten the crushed out end. "Good… good," he snorted in satisfaction.

Embarrassed, Zorayda intentionally turned away from the man while trying to catch the nurse's attention, then checked herself and turned back. The man was attempting to light the butt with hands that shook uncontrollably. "Can't get this thing lit," he muttered.

"Stop it!" Zorayda snapped at him. "I gave you several packs two days ago so you wouldn't scrounge for butts." He looked up at her without a hint of recognition. At that moment, I realized it was Bob.

"Smoked 'em all. Did you bring more? When am I goin' home?"

"When the doctors say you can, Bob."

Bob's match lit the end of the butt in a random hit. He took two long desperate drags before the remnant of tobacco extinguished itself against the filter. "What'd the doctors say… take me home… "

"Bob, Fr. Doug came with me to see you."

"Take me home… did ya bring smokes?" he muttered thoughtlessly, generating a piercing stare from his wife.

"Put the cigarette out, Bob, so we can go to your room and visit."

Bob sucked again on the butt to no avail, then dropped it on the floor and crushed it with his right bunny. "You bring cigarettes?'

"Yes," Zorayda conceded. "They're in my purse. I'll give them to you when we're in your room." For the first time in the conversation, Bob looked straight at his wife and gave her a feeble smile.

"Good to see you, Dear."

"Just because I brought your smokes."

"That, too…" he said, taking her hand as he turned and shuffled toward the room shared with three other male patients, all of whom were out. As we walked down the corridor together, Zorayda turned and leaned in close to me to speak confidentially, "Bob had electric shock therapy three days ago. They might as well hit him in the head with a baseball bat. It would achieve the same result. He's still pretty scattered."

Bob sat on the edge of his bed dangling his bunny feet, inviting us to pull up two chairs.

"Great slippers, Bob," I offered.

"Think so? I got them from the lost and found. Kinda cheerful. Kinda crazy. Kinda appropriate." Although his tone was gentle, his sarcasm exposed underlying anger that exerted itself through layers of medication. "I'm not as out of it as Zorayda thinks I am," he asserted with a hint of defiance, revealing that he'd heard her comments to me on the way to the room. "I can be just as crazy as the next guy."

Zorayda moved from her chair to sit beside Bob on the bed, taking his hand in hers while recounting for him the latest Shelby news. We'd been in Bob's room for nearly a half hour when he abruptly announced that he was tired and wanted to take a nap. Zorayda removed his bunny slippers. "You know that these things aren't coming home with you, Bob," she teased as she helped him beneath the covers.

"Father, would you please pray for us," Zorayda asked.

"Would that be all right, Bob?" I questioned, seeking his permission.

He nodded his assent and took his wife's hand as I removed a small leather-bound 1928 _Book of Common Prayer_ from my pocket and thumbed through the pages for the appropriate prayer. As I began to read, Bob gave a deep sigh and looked straight into my eyes, "Doug, please don't read from the book. Pray a prayer from your heart."

"Bob, I'm not very good at that sort of thing. Seminary didn't teach us how to do that," I confessed nervously with a hint of defensiveness. I'd never prayed for another person in their presence or out loud.

"They shouldn't have to," Bob asserted. "Prayer should flow from your heartfelt love of Jesus and His love for you. The first time I prayed for a sick friend, I didn't have a clue as to what I was doing. I just jumped into the deep water. Jesus taught me to pray from my heart, not from a book or my head. At first, all I could do was float, but it wasn't long before I was taking powerful strokes in prayer. Jesus will do the same for you. Just jump in with your whole heart."

Stunned, I let my prayer book fall to the floor with a soft thud. Bob, this drugged out psych patient, who only moments ago had been disoriented and scrounging for cigarette butts, was now lucid, counseling me with wisdom and challenging advice. I never expected a man such as

Bob to be capable of being God's messenger to me. In Bob's weakness, God was made strong.[6]

I drew in a deep breath, "You're a wise and faithful man, Bob. I trust your counsel, so here goes... Dear Father, You love Bob and Zorayda." I began haltingly as if I were writing a letter, "You love them even more than they love one another. Out of the abundance of Your love, I ask You to comfort and strengthen them in this difficult time." I took another breath to press ahead, fully aware that God's Spirit was praying through me. "Please heal Bob's soul and fill him with Your peace that passes all understanding. St. Paul promised that those who believe in You, Jesus, would have the mind of Christ. I ask for the mind of Christ for Bob. Heal him so that he can go home and be with Zorayda. Please Lord. Amen."

As I finished, tears began to fall down my cheeks. Bob took my hand that rested on the side of the bed and placed it on his forehead, covering my hand with his. The heat radiating from Bob's forehead alarmed me. He felt like he was burning up with fever. I realized that my hand was trembling. I couldn't tell if the heat was emanating from Bob's head, my hand, or God's Spirit.

"Father, please bless us," Bob requested.

Through my tears I could see tears falling from the corners of Bob's eyes. Zorayda's tears were falling on Bob's other hand, which she clutched against her heart. The Holy Spirit nudged me to pray, "Father God, in the holy Name of Jesus and by the Victory of His Cross, I bless Bob and

---

6   1 Corinthians 1:25 & 2 Corinthians 12:10

Zorayda: full measure, richly, extravagantly, with love, mercy and grace."

"Amen." Bob whispered, "and thank you. God is so good, and you were faithful," he assured me, releasing my hand from his forehead. When I lifted my hand, the fiery heat immediately ceased.

"Father, did you bring Holy Oil for anointing the sick?"

"No, I'm sorry. I didn't."

"Next time," he instructed. "It's a sign of the presence of God's Spirit."

"I will. Thank you Bob, you've taught me a lot in a short time," I assured him, leaning over and giving him a gentle hug. I left the room to give Bob and Zorayda some private time together. Sinking into a chair near the nurses' desk, I was overwhelmed with gratitude and awe for God's grace.

I had prayed and blessed extemporaneously for the first time. Both were obviously of God's authorship and very little of my knowledge or skill. It was the Holy Spirit's doing. Never again would I leave home or church without Holy Oil. Through humble people, members of a failing small town church, God was teaching me how to do pastoral ministry.

Despite Zorayda's adamant protests, Bob remained under lock and key at Riverside Hospital for nearly a month before he was released into his wife's care. At home, Bob eventually returned to his retirement practice of visiting the sick and shut-in. Bob sat with them, carried on conversations, read to them from their books or his Bible, and never left a person without a prayer and blessing that included anointing with Holy Oil. "Isn't that the pastor's role?" I puzzled. Again God was convicting me, not through Bob's words this time, but his actions. He was functioning as one of Jesus' "priesthood of believers".[7] I remembered that Jesus had said, *"Very truly I tell you, whoever believes in me will do the works I have been doing, and they will do even greater things than these, because I am going to the Father."*[8]

Through this brief awkward experience of worship with Zorayda and Bob at the hospital and as their pastor at St. Mark's, the Lord was inviting me to come into His presence more regularly. He was welcoming me to sit at His feet and learn, while strengthening the foundation that He had established in my life long ago. His invitation was clear, "Come." Only in prayer and worship in His presence would I learn to become the priest He intended me to be, *"... that he who began a good work in you will carry it on to completion until the day of Christ Jesus."*[9]

The Lord had made three invitations to me filled with welcome, love and grace. Each was troubling and occurred in places that I least expected. First, the Lord Jesus invited me to accept Him as my personal Savior and Lord at the shopping center revival. Second, on Route 71 to Cleveland, Jesus invited me to surrender all of my life to Him and to trust Him to fulfill His call on my life. Third, in a time of worship with Bob and Zorayda, Jesus invited me to listen to the Holy Spirit for peoples' needs, and then pray face to face and out loud.

---

7   1 Peter 2:9
8   John 14:12
9   Philippians 1:6

You may find these stories disquieting. What I discovered was that my acceptance of each invitation moved me forward in the process of becoming who God purposed me to be. As you continue reading, He may be gently nudging you forward, too.

PART II

INVITATIONS JESUS MADE

IN ADDITION to the foundational invitation of salvation, Jesus made many other kinds of invitations. The invitations were typical of the invitations Jesus offers us today. He issued invitations to the disciples, the curious, the needy, and those seeking a blessing. He invited people to fellowship with Him around food and conversation. As crowds pressed in upon Him and religious rulers intensified opposition to His ministry, Jesus invited His disciples to come away with Him for quiet and rest. Jesus' invitations were not without conditions and often entailed sacrifice. This was especially true when He invited all who wanted to be His disciples to take up their cross and follow Him.[10]

In this section are explanations of six types of invitations Jesus made and the possible consequences of accepting His invitations. The lessons I learned from these invitations are illustrated by a number of stories from the three congregations I served: Church of the Epiphany, Euclid, Ohio; St. Mark's Episcopal Church, Shelby, Ohio; and Christ The King Church, Campbell, California. Two of the stories are from First Presbyterian Church in Ambler, Pennsylvania, where Eleanor and I worship in our retirement. All the stories are shared with permission or names have been changed.

---

10   Mark 8:34

1. "COME, AND YOU WILL SEE...."

Jesus often issued invitations for people to *"Come, and you will see...."*[11] He understood that many people invested considerable time and walked great distances to see and hear Him. They came because He taught with astounding authority,[12] and they were looking for the promised Messiah. They sought to have their needs met through the healings, miracles and deliverance that flowed from Him. The people who came heard truth that touched their hearts. They witnessed things they had never seen before.

Even now, Jesus welcomes us with all our doubts, fears and sins to draw near to hear God's Word and see what He is doing. In church gatherings, the absence of Holy Spirit authored invitations, like those made by Jesus and His disciples, denies people the opportunity to see and experience what God is doing in their lives and in the world around them.

Sunday worship in most churches is devoted to hearing God's Word read and proclaimed. We hear, but we don't often see. The church has become solely an ear, hearing without the opportunity to process what we've heard, either intellectually or experientially. Prayerful interaction with God helps us assimilate what we've heard, but in corporate gatherings, time is seldom allotted for this process. Invitations facilitate interaction with God, which can unfold in times of worship, fellowship, and quiet prayer.

---

11   John 1:39
12   Matthew 7:29

Story: Elsie's Vision for St. Mark's

St. Mark's Episcopal Church had been purchased as a build-it-yourself kit from Sears in the early 1920's. A steep roof was topped with a Celtic cross. The building was sided with cedar shingles painted concrete gray with white trim. Because stained glass was a luxury beyond the parish budget, the windows were simple amber glass. The double front doors were a bright, welcoming red that had unfortunately failed to produce many visitors, let alone new members.

A little more than a year into my first pastorate, St. Mark's held an annual meeting that was less about the tight budget and more about a "way forward" - the contemporary diocesan term denoting God's vision for the congregation. The conversation was animated, but largely focused on past failures rather than strategies for an anticipated future. "We tried that, and it didn't work" - the seven last words of a dying church. I was becoming frustrated and impatient with the meeting.

Then Elsie Appeman, a senior member of the congregation, stood to speak, "Father Doug, I've been a member of this parish all my life. I've prayed for St. Mark's every day, even when I was a child. I've always known that God has a purpose for this parish, but we never seem to get a foothold on His path for us. Just before you arrived, I was crying out to God to bless this little parish. 'I don't have a lot of time left,' I told Him. 'If you're going to answer my prayers, it had better be soon,'" Elsie laughed. "This is going to sound strange... "

She had captured everyone's attention. "Go ahead, Elsie," I urged.

"I was kneeling up there," she pointed toward the front pew, "talking to the Lord. All of a sudden He was standing beside me and asked me to take His hand. Before I knew what was happening, we were above the church, maybe a hundred feet, and I could see through the roof into the nave and sanctuary. St. Mark's was filled with people. Some were even standing at the front door stoop to participate in worship. People's arms were raised in praise and adoration. The music was glorious — hymns I recognized and choruses of praise. Tears filled my eyes as I felt the Lord's arm around me, 'Elsie, before you come home, you will see this come to pass at St. Mark's. Your prayers and the prayers of many others are being answered.' Before I knew it I was back here kneeling in prayer."

One after another, people at the meeting knelt in silent prayer. After a few moments one of the choir members began to sing the Doxology and was joined by the congregation. Elsie raised her arms in praise. At that moment I knew that St. Mark's would never be the same, and neither would I.

It would be great to tell you that we clearly knew the next steps, but we didn't have a clue. Surprisingly, although St. Mark's was a small struggling parish, we had an active youth group. Several parish teenagers heard about an exciting youth ministry at St. Luke's Episcopal Church in Bath, Ohio, an hour and a half drive up Route 71 from Shelby. A season of cajoling was finally rewarded with an adult who was willing to drive a carload of youth to see what was going on with the young people at St. Luke's.

They came back excited enough to return to St. Luke's youth group several more times. That's not all. St. Mark's youth began to urge their parents and other adult parishioners to check out St. Luke's Wednesday night worship. "You should see what's happening. It's amazing!" the young people encouraged. It sounded to me like Rick's urging me to attend the revival at the Bay Village shopping center.

The first carload of adults was filled with an atmosphere of suspicion and anxiety as it pulled into the parking lot at St. Luke's, a gray-shingled building with white trim and a brilliant red door just like St. Mark's. What had once been the place of worship was now the fellowship hall of a much larger parish.

On the way home the car was filled with excitement. In time St. Mark's invited Fr. Chuck Irish, his Associate Pastor, Fr. Bob Hansen, and a contingent of St. Luke's parishioners to spend several days of fellowship and ministry at St. Mark's. It was a new beginning for the parish. The old mantra of "We did it, and it didn't work" was thankfully replaced with, "By God's grace we can do this."

Elsie's prophetic vision started a new life not only for the parish, but for her personal life as well. She was an eighty-five year old woman who had never married. As a young woman she had worked for a young man, John Hogsette, who became her dear friend. He was happily married and beginning a family. They kept in touch with one another over the years by exchanging Christmas cards with brief notes, catching up on one another's progress through life.

As Elsie was preparing to celebrate her eighty-sixth Christmas, she received the traditional card from John. The note read, "Elsie, my dear wife, Jane, died last February after a long, agonizing bout with cancer. My children have grown, married, and are occupied with their own families and careers. I'd like to see you, so we can catch up after all these years."

Elsie invited John to lunch at the mall, just to catch up with one another. He invited her to dinner the next day to catch-up some more. They agreed to have dinner together Saturday evening, some place fancy, still catching up. With all the "catching-up" their friendship quickly blossomed into something much deeper. John proposed.

The Hogsettes' wedding was the embodiment of the vision God had given Elsie of a vibrant parish life that was beginning to unfold. St. Mark's was overflowing with worshippers, many with raised hands and voices in exuberant praise. Joy was palpable for the Lord and for John and Elsie. What Elsie had seen in the spirit, she and all in attendance experienced in the flesh.

Jesus invites us to come and see. The people at St. Mark's saw a failing parish, but Jesus invited Elsie to see the parish as it would become. In Bath, St. Mark's parishioners saw and experienced the reality of exciting worship that would eventually be theirs. When the parish accepted Jesus' invitation to come and see, they were given a vision filled with promise, hope, and a purposeful future.

Today we see congregations with a dwindling membership of senior believers. Many churches have closed, only to be turned into housing, bookstores, and bars. More churches face this fate. Surely the Holy Spirit would have us see and embrace a different future for the Church. The needs of people are more numerous and greater than ever, yet we have failed to issue Jesus' invitations which would enable us to see and, through the Holy Spirit, do the things Jesus did and even greater things.

2. "COME TO ME, ALL YOU WHO ARE WEARY AND BURDENED...."

The second kind of invitation is to the weary in body, soul and spirit. Jesus' presence communicated a non-verbal welcome to everyone in need. People brought, *"... all who were ill with various diseases, those suffering severe pain, the demon-possessed, those having seizures, and the paralyzed; and he healed them."* [13] His invitations were filled with understanding and compassion: *"Come to me, all you who are weary and burdened, and I will give you rest."* [14] Jesus

---

13   Matthew 4:24
14   Matthew 11:28

still reaches out to us today, inviting us to draw near for His healing touch through the sovereign power of the Holy Spirit, and the hearts, hands and prayers of brothers and sisters in Christ.

In church, the burdens that people bring usually go unaddressed. They frequently leave the service just as weary as when they entered. Interactive invitations enable people to come into God's presence where they can have their needs addressed in prayer, be blessed, and have their burdens lifted. Being in Jesus' presence was the main reason people walked great distances and brought their needy friends. His healing, miracles, deliverance, and forgiveness free us from wearying burdens.

Story: Oakland Stadium Event

The Oakland Stadium hosted a Promise Keepers Conference in 1995 focused on the theme "Raise the Standard." On a Saturday morning, 70,000 men filled the football stadium to capacity. Bands and vocalists saturated the environment with songs of praise and worship. Hundreds of helium balloons ascended heavenward, and multi-colored beach balls bounced from the balconies to the field and back in an enthusiastic and joyful spirit of anticipation. Forty-three men from Christ the King Church had carpooled to the event with great anticipation.

Coach Bill McCartney welcomed the huge gathering of men into the presence of the Lord Jesus Christ. It took a while for the collective energy to become focused and the last balloon to be released. The Coach repeated his welcome and then made an invitation for men who were exhausted, discouraged, and floundering in their faith to come forward for prayer and recommit their lives to Jesus Christ. "Let's prepare ourselves for all that God has for us in our time together in His presence."

The men from our group were seated in the second balcony at about the fifty-yard line. Men in the folding chairs on the field began to respond to the invitation in huge numbers. As we looked around the stadium, the aisles in the stands and balconies were jam-packed with men trying to reach the stage and stand before a huge wooden Cross. The Christ the King men gave up trying to reach the stage and stood in the aisle facing the speaker: men with tears running down their cheeks; men with their hands in the air; men falling to their knees on the hard pavement of the second and third balconies.

Some men in our group were invited guests who came out of curiosity, to honor a friendship, or to please their wife. Several of those men were standing in response to the Coach's invitation, "Come to the Lord Jesus, all you men who are weary and burdened for any reason." A simple invitation offered with compassion and promise identified real needs, lifted burdens and weariness, and drew a multitude of men closer to Jesus.

3. BLESSINGS

A third type of invitation that was a vital part of Jesus' ministry was for people to receive a blessing. In the Old Covenant, God blessed Abraham to be a blessing to a multitude. In the New Testament, people brought little children to Jesus for a blessing. This troubled the disciples who saw the request as a nuisance. Jesus said, *"Let the little children come to me, and do not hinder them, for the kingdom of heaven belongs to such as these."* [15]

Today, Jesus not only blesses infants and children, He blesses you and me to be a blessing to others. Being blessed by God and giving God's blessing begins as soon as we accept Jesus' invitation to *"come and follow."* You and I are a new creation, a chosen people, a royal priesthood, a holy nation[16] blessed by God the Father and invited to take up our inheritance of the promised kingdom.[17]

Story: Prayer for a Neighbor

The sole purpose of a lighthouse is to save lives. Originally during foul weather, huge watch fires were ignited atop points of land to guide ships. Over time the fires were replaced by lighthouses which shine their light above the water and below the fog, piercing the darkness, warning of danger, and guiding to safety. Jesus said, *"I am the light of the world. Whoever follows me will never walk in darkness, but will have the light of life."* [18] His light is magnified through His believers to the world, especially our primary mission field – the place where we live. This is what He commanded: *"I have made you a light for the Gentiles, that you may bring salvation to the ends of the earth."* [19] Believers in Christ are lighthouses to the places where they live and work.

---

15   Matthew 19:14-15
16   1 Peter 2:9
17   Matthew 25:34
18   John 8:12
19   Acts 13:47

Christ the King Church became part of a Santa Clara countywide prayer evangelism movement called "Lighthouses of Prayer", which followed the sequence Jesus taught His disciples: bring peace and give blessings; build relationships; pray for the sick and be of service; proclaim the Good News of Jesus Christ.[20]

The "Lighthouses of Prayer" ministry gave Christians a concrete way to go into the world and share the Gospel with everyone. More specifically, it gave believers a way to go into their neighborhood, work, school, and places of recreation with the Good News. It was more a lifestyle than a program. The commitment to prayer is sustained by keeping it simple. It's Christians talking to God about their neighbors before talking to their neighbors about God. Daily blessing prayer trusts the Holy Spirit to work in peoples' hearts. Oswald Chambers said, "Prayer does not fit us for the greater work; prayer is the greater work."

My neighbor, Tom, was the catalyst that formed our collection of homes into a neighborhood. Tom knew everyone and all the latest scuttlebutt. Building on Tom's existing relationship with the neighbors, I partnered with him to be a lighthouse of prayer. That meant that I prayed daily for the nine homes I could see from my front door.

One evening while putting out the garbage, I encountered my neighbors, Tom and Alden, performing the same chore. As we greeted one another and struck up a conversation, Alden off-handedly mentioned that he was going to the hospital in a few days for catheterization and possible

---

20   Luke 10:5-9

angioplasty. "Alden, would you let us pray for you, right here?" I asked.

"I guess that would be OK."

Tom attended St. Lucy's Roman Catholic Church, and Alden was a lapsed Southern Baptist. "Would you allow Tom to put his hand over your heart?" I asked.

"Sure."

The prayer was brief. Tom's hand trembled. I was praying with my eyes open, so when Alden began to lose his balance I was ready to help him remain stable.

"Wooo! That was something else!" Alden exclaimed. "Maybe I won't have to go to the hospital after all. Maybe I ought to go back to church."

I urged him to give his doctor the privilege of confirming the healing. He did, and God received the glory. Alden also returned to church. More glory to God!

My wife and I were committed to be a blessing in our neighborhood by praying for our neighbors. We also prayed with one another, often asking God's blessing on our marriage, parenting, and careers. In the morning on school days, our son stood at the front door as we placed our hands on his shoulders and prayed for God's blessing on him and his day. At church I discovered that many parents had never blessed one another or their children with prayers of hope and promise.

I don't think what I found among my parishioners was unique to them or unusual in our culture, even among Christians. That insight brought conviction. The Lord prompted me to invite parents to come forward to the communion table and pray for one another and their children. Children were given invitations to pray blessings upon their parents. Grandparents were invited to pray for their sons and daughters and their grandchildren. The need was clearly apparent. The invitation was made with little risk.

4. FOOD AND CONVERSATION

A fourth type of invitation is for food and conversation. The climax of Jesus' invitation to food and fellowship was the Last Supper, but He both issued and accepted many others. He often rested at the home of Lazarus and his sisters, Mary and Martha. Simon, a Pharisee, invited Jesus to dinner.[21] Jesus invited Himself into the home of a new acquaintance, Zacchaeus.[22] The Pharisees criticized Jesus for eating with tax collectors and sinners. They accused Him of being a glutton and drunkard.[23] Twice, Jesus miraculously fed thousands of people who had traveled far and stayed long to hear Him preach. He multiplied a few loaves of bread and several fish to satisfy everyone's hunger. After His crucifixion and resurrection, some of the disciples had returned to fishing on the Sea of Galilee. The risen Jesus cooked a meal on the beach and said: *"Come and have breakfast."*[24] It is clear that Jesus infuses the breaking of bread and eating together with a greater importance than simple physical sustenance.

---

21   Luke 7:36-50
22   Luke 19:1-10
23   Matthew 11:19
24   John 21:12

Inviting people to break bread together is essential to both church life and evangelism. Sharing conversation over coffee or a meal enriches fellowship and provides an opportunity to identify needs, share faith, and pray. It's one of the things the church is supposed to be about, *"They devoted themselves to the apostles' teaching and to fellowship, to the breaking of bread and to prayer."*[25] Jesus is truly made known through the breaking of bread.

Story: Welcoming Goliath

The Rev. Bob Hansen had been the assistant pastor at St. Luke's in Bath, Ohio. He became a mentor and close friend. Bob and his wife Mary Carol eventually moved to Gilroy, California where he became the rector of St. Stephen's Episcopal Church. He introduced me to Shannon Mallory, the first bishop of the newly formed Diocese of El Camino Real. Bishop Mallory invited me to become the vicar of a failing mission, St. Lawrence the Martyr Episcopal Church, a.k.a. Christ the King, in Campbell, CA.

---

25   Acts 2:42

Bob's wife, Mary Carol, was an accredited Marriage, Family, and Child Counselor. At her husband's and my urging, she established a Christian counseling center at St. Lawrence. Although a brilliant therapist and gifted teacher, Mary Carol was mildly introverted and had a wry sense of humor. Given her somber demeanor, it was incongruous that she loved line dancing, a passion she both pursued and introduced to the church at parking lot picnics. Shedding her introversion, she became our cowgirl dance instructor. Patio lights, hamburgers, soft drinks, and country western music entertained parishioners, neighbors and passersby late into the evening.

The Wednesday before the Saturday picnic, I sat looking out the window of my second floor office at Mt. Hamilton, breathing the pollen-saturated, sinus-irritating, eye-watering air. California's beauty comes with a price! The phone rang, breaking my mental drift. A woman had found the mission's number in the directory and wanted to know if she could see me within the hour. Considering that St.

Lawrence could only afford the standard two-line yellow page listing, her finding us among the dozens of churches with much more elaborate ads had to be a God thing.

Paulette Douglas arrived fifteen minutes later, "I was closer than I thought," she explained. Paulette was in her mid-thirties. Her brunette hair softly framed her gentle features. Her infectious smile was punctuated with the deepest dimples I'd ever seen. She was dressed in a business suit appropriate for her job as a sales representative for Bell Communication Systems.

People who look up clergy in the phone book aren't doing so out of idle curiosity. Paulette needed help. She was desperate, carrying an overwhelming burden. "I've been dating a man for the past two years. We love one another. It's just that he doesn't seem to want to go the next step," she confided.

"What do you think the next step is?"

"Well, I'm in my thirties. My biological clock is ticking. I was hoping he'd ask me to marry him, but he has trouble saying he loves me. I don't know what to do. I feel stuck," she sighed.

"Paulette, have you prayed about your relationship?"

"Yes, but I don't seem to get any answers. Randall claims to be an atheist. He's not hostile to Christianity, just indifferent," she shared.

"How about you?"

"I'm sort of an Episcopalian. I went to church for a while in my teens."

"There's a possible explanation for God's silence to your prayers. The Bible says that no one can come to the Father but through Jesus Christ. God is waiting for you to come into a personal relationship with His Son, Jesus."

"If I did that, there would be an even greater distance between Randall and me. I don't know…" she said, anxiety rising in her voice.

"It's possible that your relationship with Jesus will be a witness to Randall, drawing him to the Lord and you. You already love God and are seeking His best for your life. God knows your heart and cares for you or you wouldn't be here," I explained.

"What should I do?"

"I can't tell you that. What is the Lord saying to you?"

We were quiet. Outside, junior high students walked home from school, teasing and taunting one another.

"How do I bring Jesus into my life?" Paulette asked with tears in her eyes.

"You just did," I assured her. We prayed together an extemporaneous "sinner's prayer." I heard her confession of sin, pronounced God's forgiveness, and asked for the indwelling of the Holy Spirit. As we prayed, the burden visibly lifted off Paulette's shoulders.

"What should I do next?" she asked.

"Invite Randall to come with you this Saturday evening to a picnic in the church parking lot. There will be good food, ice cream, and line dancing. No preaching, teaching, or worship to put him off. And don't tell him about Jesus, just pray God's blessing on him in your private prayers. Assure Randall that he'll have a good time," I urged.

"I can do that. Thank you. Thank you so much!" She gave me a hug.

Surprisingly, Randall accepted Paulette's invitation. He was a Philistine, all 6' 5" and 265 pounds of him. Everyone felt like David in his presence. The gentle, extroverted giant came more for the food and ice cream than the line dancing. Before the evening was over, Randall had met everyone, remembered their names and a little bit about them. We knew this because Randall came to worship the next morning with Paulette and greeted everyone by name and with a tidbit of what they'd shared.

Randall told me, "Doug, I had a great time last night. Everyone was so warm and welcoming. I'm around people everyday who are working some kind of deal or pushing some agenda. Last night I felt at home and actually relaxed. This is a great group of people. I'll be back."

Two weeks later Randall made an appointment. He entered my office, gave me a bear hug, sat down and said, "I'm here to find out about Jesus." He left having given his life to the Lord. He also made his first confession, unloading some very burdensome sins. Two and a half hours later, Randall was a new man. Within a month, he had read the Bible from cover to cover.

Several months later, on a Sunday morning before the congregation, Randall asked Paulette to marry him. She said, "Yes" as he placed an engagement ring on her finger. Together they promised to observe a holy engagement as they prepared to become husband and wife. The congregation stood in applause. I prayed God's blessing on the betrothed, as everyone extended their hands in the couple's direction.

The congregation warmly welcomed Paulette and Randall into their midst. In turn, Paulette and Randall invited the entire congregation to their wedding. They had become family in the Body of Christ and eventually became beloved home pastors.

Invitations are an essential part of hospitality. The size of a congregation's membership, budget, facilities, or technology does not ensure that the church is welcoming. A church's hospitality is a reflection of the congregation's faith and character.

5. "COME WITH ME BY YOURSELVES TO A QUIET PLACE AND GET SOME REST."

A fifth type of invitation that Jesus offered was for quiet and rest. The press of people who sought to experience Jesus' ministry was both intense and exhausting: *". . . so many people were coming and going that they* (the disciples) *did not even have a chance to eat, he said to them, 'Come with me by yourselves to a quiet place and get some rest.'"* [26] Jesus was deeply sensitive to the burden and exhaustion caused by the opposition of the Jewish leaders, the Roman occupation, and the demands of His ministry. Burnout may not have been a diagnosis in Jesus' day, but He knew the destructive dynamic caused by a lack of physical rest and spiritual refreshment. He understood that if He and His disciples did not come apart, they would soon fall apart.

26   Mark 6:31 addition mine

Today, Jesus invites you and me to observe the Sabbath, a day of rest. In addition, He invites us to spend quiet time with Him in order to be refreshed and hear His guidance. It is essential for us to accept these invitations for the sake of our wellbeing. Quiet and rest are often a prelude to a deeper relationship with God and one another. They are also essential for us to be refreshed and alert for participation in His ministry and mission.

Story: Knights of the Golden Sword

My challenge as the pastor of Christ the King Church was to mentor Godly character in my brothers and sisters in Christ who lived under the relentless 24/7 pressures of the Silicon Valley.

At our weekly prayer breakfast the men had read _The Hidden Value of a Man_ by Gary Smalley and John T. Trent. The premise of the book is that men have the ability to wield two swords: one silver, one gold. At home, a man uses the golden sword to bless his spouse and children. The silver sword that is used in the business world is less loving and intimate. The men responded to this teaching by founding the Brotherhood of the Golden Sword to encourage deeper intimacy in their families. The Brotherhood met monthly and sponsored an annual men's retreat. Saturday afternoon of the retreats was set aside for recreation that was intentionally outrageous. Activities began with the annual Knights of the Golden Sword parade and tournament. Each knight came dressed in homemade armor, featuring the creative use of garbage can lids, assorted athletic gear, and various colors of tights that restrained middle-aged

"love handles." Every knight's armor bore his coat of arms and name: Good Knight, All Knight, Knight and Day, Italian Knight, Pink Knight, Nighty Knight, etc. The parade to the playing field was a colorful, rowdy event surpassed only by the tournament itself.

"Pillow Polo" was played with a sponge rubber ball. Each player was equipped with a sponge-covered club that looked like a giant Q-tip. Two teams played on a soccer field. The object was to drive the ball into the opposition's net. "Pillow Polo," as played by the Brotherhood, differed from soccer in that it was completely devoid of rules. Men, vigorously going after one another with clubs, made the ball the safest thing on the field.

One such scrimmage produced a melee of pushing, shoving, laughter and flailing clubs. Tom, the Pink Knight, emerged from the chaos carried by three large knights. He appeared to be in his third trimester of pregnancy. The sponge ball had been stuffed into his pink leotards. The trio lumbered down the field and pitched the pregnant knight into the goal, scoring the first point of the tournament.

Adult males manifesting frivolous, outrageous, over-the-top behavior! What we knew was that in a stress-filled culture, people lose the ability to play. "All work and no play" robs families of a sense of adventure, fun and refreshment. Christ the King Church valued fun and rest in the midst of doing the serious work of proclaiming the Good News. We accepted the Lord's invitation to come apart, to keep us from falling apart.

Laughter and rest build Christian fellowship that can open the way to address deeper issues in our lives. It was a truth soon to be written on my heart.

Story: Oakmeal Fellowship

For twenty-three years, the men of the church had met at 6:30 A.M. every Friday morning regardless of weather, earthquakes, or holidays to eat oatmeal, say the Pledge of Allegiance, read aloud Christian books, share their thoughts, and pray. Fred was infamous for mispronouncing words and being resistant to correction. He gave birth to the Oakmeal Fellowship. Complain about the "oakmeal" and you were the next cook until death or another guy complained. "This stuff tastes like dog food!" made you the next chef. "This stuff tastes like dog food, but 'good' dog food!" kept you safe for another week. Over the years, dozens of men who passed through the Oakmeal Fellowship found a place of quiet, put aside their competitive bent, and built friendships with the Lord and their brothers in Christ.

It was the spring of 1996. For a second time, we were reading Alan Redpath's _The Making of a Man of God_. The morning's chapter focused on the character attributes of a Christian. The reading had been convicting. After an awkward silence, Fred looked down the table at Tom and said, "I know you're a Christian, but if I'm honest, there is little about you that reveals Jesus." What followed was a measured and withering critique of Tom's failings as a Christian in his brother's estimation. It was something that had been hidden in Fred's heart for a long time.

Everyone around the table expected at least a verbal altercation or for Tom to leave in a fit of anger. Instead, Tom sat up straight in his chair, pushed his empty "oak-meal" bowl away, folded his hands on the table, and looked directly at the man who was upbraiding him.

When Fred was finished speaking, Tom readjusted himself in his chair and said, "Thank you. I needed to hear that." Pausing, Tom cleared his throat before continuing, "I know I can be difficult, even abrasive. As a result people keep their distance from me, which allows me to be even more difficult. I know this is not a blessing to my brothers and sisters in Christ. It certainly is a burden to my wife and sons. And it sure doesn't help my witness or glorify the Lord. If you or any of my brothers here at the table have anything to add, I want to hear it and be held accountable by you so that I can grow in Christian character."

There were gasps of relief from men who had been holding their breath. Two brothers had tears in their eyes. Fred, who had leveled the harsh words at Tom, was visibly taken aback. In that moment we not only witnessed, we experienced, the humility required for the making of a man of God. Tom embarked on a journey of change, as did many of the men at the table, including Fred who had initiated the confrontation. It was a significant moment in the sanctification of everyone around the table.

On retreat and in weekly breakfast fellowship, men entered God's provision of rest and quiet. Jesus' invitation to join Him in this is essential to the process of our becoming who God purposes us to be. Participation in the fellowship of small groups is an important way of actively growing in Christian character. Tom and Fred experienced that. Sanctification isn't easy and is often costly. It is also necessary for our maturity as Christ's ambassadors.

Story: A Moment of Silence

Early on a Saturday morning, I was cloistered in my office seeking the Lord's direction for Sunday's sermon. Robert, a parishioner, popped his head through the open door, "Hey Doug, I was just out for a morning walk and thought I'd stop into church and say 'Hi' to the Lord. Your door was open, so 'Hi' to you, too. You got a minute?"

"Sure, come on in. What's up?"

"I'll spare you the B.S. and jump right in. I was just wondering why our worship is so full of noise: you talking, parishioners responding, the music ministry leading us in songs of praise. There's always something. We're full of noise and never quiet."

I could feel myself tensing up and becoming defensive. "That's the liturgical worship of the *Book of Common Prayer*," I offered as an explanation.

"Yeah, but when we do the intercessions, you don't even allow thirty seconds of silence. There's no room for us to add our own prayers," he said, setting forth his argument.

Sitting back in my chair, I stretched away from Robert in silence. After a moment, I leaned forward, "All right, I'll prayerfully consider what you're telling me. You have a point."

"Good, that's all I'm asking. You listen to the Lord. I know He'll talk to you about it." He smiled as he rose from his chair, "You're busy. Sorry to interrupt. I'll let you get back to it."

Throughout the day Robert's words continued to echo in my head interrupting my thoughts about the next day's sermon based on the sixth chapter of Mark in which Jesus walks on the troubled water of the Sea of Galilee.[27] Jesus had attempted unsuccessfully to find a place of quiet away from the crowds to pray and rest with His disciples, *"Come with me by yourselves to a quiet place and get some rest."*[28] Three times He sought quiet for His disciples. Three times! Obviously, Jesus felt that quiet was crucial to spiritual and mental health. That was not the point I had intended to make in my sermon, but it seemed to be the Holy Spirit's leading through Scripture and Robert's words. I threw up my arms in surrender, "I get it, Lord. I'm sorry I'm so stubborn. Please forgive me. I'll follow Your lead."

---

27   Mark 6:30-56
28   Mark 6:31

That Sunday, smiling faces and laughter filled the church. Warm hand shakes and embraces were a pre-service passing of The Peace in anticipation of worship. My brief message focused on the quiet Jesus had sought for Himself and His disciples. During the prayers of intercession, I invited worshippers to observe three minutes of 'quiet' to rest in God's presence. I suggested they offer Him their own prayer concerns, reflect on the Scripture lessons, and listen for the Lord's voice.

After the Words of Dismissal, I stood at the door to shake hands with people as they left the church. Many people expressed appreciation for the time of silence. As part of the parade exiting the church, Steven's six foot three inches towered over everyone else, even though he bent forward in an attempt to reduce his height. He was a physically and socially awkward "thirty-something". Although he was not a member of the parish, he was faithful in his participation in worship. Steven lowered his head to my ear, "Pastor, thank you for the three minutes of silence. I wasn't sure what to do with it, and almost got up to leave… then the Lord spoke to me. What He said touched me deeply.… . He told me that He loved me… that He wouldn't leave me… and that I'm where I'm supposed to be… right here…." While wiping tears with the back of his hand, he assured me, "I'll call you… we'll talk." He stepped away before I could reply.

I was starting to follow Steve when arms wrapped around me in a hug. Robert's smile revealed his gratitude.

"What was that about?" his wife inquired. "He doesn't usually hug people."

"We were thanking the Lord for our obedience. Robert will tell you about it on the way home."

"That'll be an interesting conversation!" she grinned.

A simple invitation to a few minutes of quiet marked the beginning of significant change in Steve's life. In time, he made a public confession of faith and became a member of the church. He traveled with mission teams to India and Mexico and served on the governing board of the church. Steve stood tall. He changed and so did we as we embraced periods of quiet in the midst of worship.

6. "REPENT" AND "COME FOLLOW ME"

Jesus, having completed His time of testing in the wilderness, began His public ministry with a brief, pointed proclamation: *"Repent, for the kingdom of heaven has come near."* [29] Repentance is an about-face from the world, the flesh and the devil. Levi was a detested tax collector who repented of his sin and left everything to follow Jesus. He held a great banquet for Jesus to meet his friends and fellow tax collectors. The Pharisees and teachers of the Law were irate. They voiced their complaints to Jesus' disciples about His associating with notorious sinners. Jesus answered them, *"It is the sick who need a doctor, not those in good health. My purpose is to invite sinners to turn from their sins, not to spend my time with those who think themselves already good enough."* [30]

29   Matthew 4:4
30   Luke 5:31-32 **The Living Bible**

Jesus' invitation to repentance had a companion invitation to discipleship, *"Come, follow me, and I will send you out to fish for men."*[31] Jesus invited ordinary fishermen, a teacher of the law, a tax collector, a rich young ruler, and many others to follow Him. Jesus attracted large crowds who came to hear His teaching. Everyone was invited. Jesus has a kingdom purpose for your life and mine, but we must accept His invitation. Everyone *is* invited!

Story: Jesus Smiled

Retirement for a "Type A" personality like me is torture. God in His grace provided me a job as a deckhand for RiverQuest, an environmental education company in Pittsburgh, Pennsylvania.

Kimberly Porr interviewed me for the position. She had been a Naval officer. Having secured a captain's license, Kim became the Operations Manager and a captain within the company's small fleet: *Voyager, Discovery,* and *Scout.* She was the first female commercial captain operating a passenger vessel on the Three Rivers. Aboard the vessels, Kim's leadership in her role and responsibilities as captain was exceptional. She solicited everyone's opinion and made firm authoritative decisions based on facts and nautical rules.

On land, Kim was attractive and approachable, but something of a train wreck. She was a single mother of five children, living with a man who was not her husband. The crew believed that it was their responsibility to watch after

---

31   Matthew 4:19

and protect her, a task that was not always appreciated by Captain Kim.

Hard rain during the night had swollen the Three Rivers. After making an early morning call to the Emsworth lock to determine the river's level and current, we made preparations for getting underway. Having completed that task, Captain Kim and I leaned over Voyager's rail to watch ducks foraging for food in the calm shallows out of the current.

"My kids are driving me crazy. You know I have five of them. The youngest is two and the oldest is a pre-teen. They're all demanding," Kim bemoaned. "And my damned boyfriend is no help."

Kim's complaints continued until the senior deckhand emerged from the engine room with a request that she join him to check out a potential problem with the starboard drive unit.

"I was going to offer to pray for you and your family right now, but Terry needs you."

"Nice thought, but I don't know what help prayer would be. I need something concrete right now," she muttered, shrugging her shoulders as she turned away in response to Terry's request.

Captain Kim's needs weighed heavily on my heart. She, her children, and boyfriend were in my prayers. As a result of our move from California to Pittsburgh, we had several items that needed a new home. One of them was from my office in Campbell. It was a large painting of Jesus' face with a neutral expression. Two days after our conversation, I gave the framed picture to Captain Kim.

"Thanks. But what am I gonna do with this?" Kim puzzled.

"I hoped that Jesus might bring you some comfort… even answer your prayers," I offered.

"Yep, that's not gonna happen," Kim grumbled. "Another thing to deal with."

A few years later, Eleanor and I moved to the Philadelphia area to be near our son and his family. During that time, Captain Kim became enmeshed in company politics and was fired. On one of our trips back to visit family in Ohio, I called Kim to ask if we could get together when we passed through Pittsburgh.

"Hey Doug, remember that picture of Jesus you gave me a long time ago?" Kim questioned.

I answered in the affirmative, but honestly, I didn't remember giving her the picture.

"You said it had been in your office in California, "she continued, sensing that I was floundering.

"Oh yeah."

"Anyhow, I hung the picture in my bedroom so I'd see it first thing in the morning. I was having a hard time with the kids. Some are teenagers. You know how hard that is! And my boy friend had left me — actually I threw him out.

"So, I'm struggling getting the kids off to school. Getting myself ready for work at Pittsburgh Cruise Line. You know I work there now? All this stuff was pulling me apart. I looked at the picture of Jesus, and He's looking back at me with a warm smile. His picture has been there for years, but I'd never seen His smile before."

I remembered the picture, but not the smile.

"It was so warm and welcoming. I threw up my hands, 'I give up. Please forgive me, Jesus.' I gave my life to Him right then and there. Jesus is my Lord and Savior. I'm going to church and teaching Sunday school. In fact, I'm what they call the Director of Christian Education. The kids go, too. And I have a new boyfriend. He's a Christian. We're working at walking the walk." Kim's enthusiasm brought joy to my heart.

Kim continued, "After my experience with Jesus, I was diagnosed with cancer. I was bedridden for six months without an income. It was only by the grace of God that my family and I got through that time physically and financially. Doug, my treatments were difficult. I prayed long and hard. Eventually I came to accept any outcome for myself. But in the times of prayer, I found that God was asking me to pray for others… relatives and friends. I was asking God to help them. This became my purpose, a purpose that gave me comfort and peace."

Kim had accepted Jesus' invitation with repentance and faith. The Lord's welcoming smile was the invitation. Kim surrendered to Him. He met her needs, healed her cancer and broken heart, gave her a new purpose and the eternal gift of salvation.

CONDITIONS, COSTS, AND REWARDS OF ACCEPTING JESUS' INVITATIONS

Jesus' invitations brim with total acceptance, but they do not come without cost and conditions. The cost is absolute surrender to God. The conditions are repentance for our sins and forgiveness. We are called to amend our lives through the guidance of the Holy Spirit and to take up our cross and follow Him. God loves us, even in our fallen state before salvation. He loves extravagantly without our having to do anything to earn or deserve His love. But our forgiveness comes with the condition that we forgive those who have sinned against us. In order to receive God's forgiveness, we must forgive. This is not an obscure biblical principle. Jesus taught it in what we know as the Lord's Prayer. A sentence in the prayer sets forth the principle: ". . .and forgive us our sins, just as we have forgiven those who have sinned against us."[32] After teaching the prayer Jesus realized that His disciples most likely didn't comprehend the principle, so He underlined it by saying, "For if you forgive other people when they sin against you, your heavenly Father will also forgive you."[33]

A young man of great faith and potential came to Jesus with questions that revealed his obedience to the Law and his passion for God. Jesus' love for the young man produced an invitation that addressed the obstacle in the man's heart that kept him from what he was seeking. "One thing you lack," Jesus said. "Go, sell everything you have and give to the poor, and you will have treasure in heaven. Then come,

32   Matthew 6:12 The Living Bible
33   Matthew 6:14-15

follow me." At this the man's face fell. He went away sad, because he had great wealth.[34] The spirit of materialism and the pleasures of the world are extremely powerful.

Just as the account of the rich young man's encounter with Jesus is recorded in all three synoptic Gospels, so are Jesus' repeated admonitions about the cost of being one of His disciples: *"Whoever wants to be my disciple must deny themselves and take up their cross daily and follow me."* [35]

There is a significant cost, but with that cost comes an incomprehensible reward: *". . .as it is written, 'No eye has seen, no ear has heard, no mind has conceived what God has prepared for those who love him....*" [36] He gives those who follow Him a purpose-filled life now and the promise of eternal life with Him in His kingdom. Jesus has prepared an inheritance and a place for His people. He is coming again, with or without our invitation. The first coming was on a lowly donkey and led to crucifixion. At the Second Coming, Jesus will be mounted on a white horse in great victory as the judge of humanity. *"The Spirit and the bride say, "Come!" And let the one who hears say, "Come!"... .He who testifies to these things says, "Yes, I am coming soon."* [37]

Story: Carl's Career

In my first year of ordained ministry, I served as a Deacon at the Church of the Epiphany, Euclid, Ohio. The rector, Fr. Bill Haas, presented me with the challenge of occasionally preaching at the main Sunday morning worship

---

34   Mark 10:21-22
35   Matthew 16:24, Mark 8:37, Luke 9:23
36   1 Corinthians 2:9
37   Revelations 22:17 & 20

service. In my second attempt from the pulpit, I focused on Paul's admonition to the Corinthians, *"Do not be misled: 'Bad company corrupts good character.' Come back to your senses as you ought, and stop sinning; for there are some who are ignorant of God—I say this to your shame."* [38]

My sermon was an awkward attempt to illustrate that Christian character is the primary component of our witness. For years in college and seminary, I had been clueless about this reality, but persistently the Lord taught me the importance of Christian character. My inattentiveness to character was sin in my life that required repentance. The Holy Spirit suggested that some of the people in church that morning might be struggling with the same thing, so I concluded the sermon by asking people to join me in the "Confession of Sin". It was out of order from the liturgy and the Sunday bulletin. Fr. Bill would not be happy.

Afterward at the front door, a longtime member of the parish thanked me for the sermon. I internally dismissed his compliment, having already given myself a failing grade. Carl seemed to sense this, because he took my elbow and led me away from the crowd at the door.

"I'm serious, Deacon. What you said about Christian character really convicted me. I work for a company that's fallen on hard times. I'm a sales representative for them, and recently they've been telling me to do things that are dishonest. As a Christian it's put me in an awful bind. Will you pray for me right now? I need God to show me what I'm supposed to do," he confided.

---

38   1 Corinthians 15:33-34

As Carl kept a tight grip on my arm, I offered a halting prayer that I remembered from the Prayer Book. Weeks later, Fr. Bill told me that Carl resigned from the company that had employed him for over two decades. Older and jobless, he was struggling in his search for work. It took Carl five months to find other, lesser employment.

God would not allow me to easily walk away from my encounter with Carl, awakening me in the night with new insight. He showed me that I had done what Jesus did in His preaching, teaching and telling of parables. He set forth a truth and gave listeners the opportunity to respond. Jesus put it in terms of loosing our self from the world, the flesh and the devil, while binding our self to the things of God.[39] Jesus invited a wealthy young man to surrender everything to follow Him. The young ruler refused the invitation.[40] Carl gave up his employment to accept Jesus' invitation to follow Him rather than the world.

Story: The Lord's Priesthood, Not Mine

Praying at St. Mark's altar rail in the early morning before the church office opened, I spoke to the Lord about the depletion of my passion for ministry. "You promised that Your joy would be my strength. I don't have any strength left. I feel flat. I'm emotionally drained," I lamented. "Jesus, without Your help I'm not sure how much longer I can do this. We've had this conversation before, and You filled me with Your Holy Spirit. I'm back again and need something more."

---

39   Matthew 16:19 & 18:18
40   Matthew 19:16-22

"Good. I've been waiting for you, Douglas. You're very tenacious and extremely stubborn. You're a lot like My friend, Elisha. It took him a long time to come to the end of himself, just like you."

"Lord, I don't understand. I'm miserable. That's what You've been waiting for?"

"Yes. Without discomfort, you wouldn't ask for help, let alone be willing to listen. Listen carefully. The priesthood for which My Father created you, called you, equipped you, ordained you, and anointed you is not yours. It is MY priesthood. I have given it to you in trust. My purpose is for you to give it away to every believer who becomes My disciple. They are the priesthood of all believers. You are holding onto the priesthood as though it belongs to you. In giving away what I've entrusted to you, the gift increases in others and in you. If you keep it for yourself, it will spoil like hoarded manna in the wilderness."

Tears of repentance rolled down my cheeks as the sword of the Lord's truth pierced me to the core, revealing the foolishness of my pride and possessiveness. I had completely missed the obvious and fallen into the narcissistic deception that the priesthood was all about me. It's not. It is all about Jesus. "I'm so terribly sorry, Jesus. Please forgive my sin of self-centeredness and taking something that isn't mine."

The Lord knew that of all the Bible's characters, Elisha was a kindred spirit of mine. God had told Elijah, His fiery spokesman to Israel's kings, that it was time to retire. This news elicited reluctant obedience from Elijah who was to anoint the farmer, Elisha, to be his successor. Elijah found Elisha with twelve teams of oxen yoked to a single-blade plow, determined to break up a field of fallow ground.[41] Elisha could have plowed sheet steel with the rig he'd assembled. This was a picture of stubbornness that God intended to sanctify for His purposes.

Jesus spoke these words into my heart, "Douglas, the prophet Elisha was stubborn, but he is my friend. You, like him, are stubborn. I forgive your sin and sanctify your stubbornness. Turn it into persistence. You, too, are My friend."

In response to the Lord's admonition, I began to teach members of the congregation how to pray for healing in body, soul and spirit. At first I shared my Oil Stock with the teams I had trained to minister at the altar rail. In three weeks, I lost three Oil Stocks. Thereafter, when I released new teams to minister, I issued them their own Oil Stocks and gave them access to the church's supply of Holy Oil.

Within Episcopal Church culture, the use of Holy Oil is the sole purview of the ordained. Word soon reached the diocesan office that members of St. Mark's, Shelby, were ministering healing prayer with the use of Holy Oil. This alone was cause for alarm, but the scuttlebutt also had it that laity, men and women, were carrying Oil Stocks in their pockets to anoint people even outside the church. A curt letter arrived at my office a month later from diocesan headquarters. The Bishop demanded that I immediately stop allowing the laity to minister healing and that I collect all the Oil Stocks that had been distributed. "Only ordained priests will administer Holy Oil within the Diocese of Ohio."

---

41   1 Kings 19:19-20

In my letter of reply, I cited my recent experience with the Lord, retelling how I had been called to account and convicted of taking ownership of the Lord's priesthood. "I've been called to be a good steward of His priesthood. My understanding is that I am not to bury this sacred trust in the ground of my own possession, but to give it away to all believers for the multiplication of His ministry." The Bishop never acknowledged my response and never held me accountable for my persistent disobedience to him. It became a spiritual "don't ask, don't tell."

What began with prayer and anointing for healing grew into teaching believers how to lead people to Jesus. I shared the ministry of teaching from God's Word by mentoring those whom God had gifted, just as the teachers at St. Mark's had mentored me. Later in California, at Christ the King Church, men and women were trained to lead home fellowship groups, share the Lord's Supper, and take Holy Communion to shut-ins. I taught parents to bless their children and children to bless their parents. During the Sunday celebration of the Lord's Supper, I invited the whole congregation to raise their hands and join in saying the prayer of blessing over bread and wine. I urged everyone to hold hands as we prayed the Lord's Prayer. Over time, I gave away what the Lord had entrusted to me. The Lord returned joy to my heart, but even more important, the Lord ignited the congregation's passion for ministry.

I gave away what God had entrusted to me as a pastor so more people would receive prayer and ministry both in the church and out in the world. I had to be realistic about the number of people I was able to pray with and minster to in a week. By giving away ministry to those who showed mature Christian character and who had been equipped for service, there was more, much more, ministry.

JESUS *IS* THE INVITATION

We have examined six types of invitations that Jesus made and the possible cost of accepting them. The foundational invitation is receiving Jesus as personal Savior and Lord. It is the most important decision a person will ever make for it is the only decision that has eternal consequences. The Gospels record many invitations Jesus made to a multitude of people, but three of His invitations highlight that Jesus *is* the invitation.

Nicodemus was a Pharisee and a member of the Sanhedrin, the ruling body of the Jewish people. Jesus knew him to be an educated man and teacher of the law. Jesus spoke to him with the authority of one who also taught the Law. Nicodemus acknowledged that Jesus was a rabbi sent from God. In acknowledging Jesus, Nicodemus ran counter to the Sanhedrin and because of this, visited Jesus under the cover of night. He came with theological questions, but Jesus saw Nicodemus' need and addressed the deepest question of his heart, *"I tell you the truth, no one can see the kingdom of God unless he is born again."*[42]

---

42   John 3:3

Nicodemus found this concept bewildering. Even so, Jesus invited him to be born again by water and the Holy Spirit. It was an invitation to Nicodemus' faith rather than his understanding. This invitation put regeneration above religion and challenged Nicodemus' faith with a profound theological truth that revealed Jesus' identity. Jesus said to Nicodemus, *"For God so loved the world that he gave his one and only Son, that whoever believes in him shall not perish but have eternal life. For God did not send his Son into the world to condemn the world, but to save the world through him."*[43]

Nicodemus accepted the life-altering invitation and became a follower of Jesus. In spite of the danger, he came to Jesus' defense by reminding his colleagues in the Sanhedrin that the law required a person be heard before being judged.[44] After Jesus' crucifixion Nicodemus provided the customary embalming spices and assisted Joseph of Arimathea in preparing the body of Jesus for burial.[45]

A second illustration of Jesus being the invitation is the story of the Samaritan woman. Jesus meets her at Jacob's well outside the town of Sycar. In Jesus' day the most direct route from Judea to Galilee was through Samaria. Because of the bitter enmity between the Jews and Samaritans, most Jews chose to go around Samaria. Therefore, the presence of Jesus and His disciples in Sychar was unusual. Jesus was tired from the long walk and noonday heat. He was both human and divine, but in this instance His humanity was

---

43   John 3:16-17
44   John 7:50-51
45   John 19:39-42

more evident. The disciples had gone into town to purchase food while Jesus rested.

It was the women's task to fetch water at the local well. Because this was such hard work, women normally went in the early morning when the day was cool. But the woman Jesus encountered had come to the well at noon in the heat of the day because the community knew her sin and had rejected her. She isolated herself to avoid their criticism and disdain.

Jesus asks her, *"Will you give me a drink?"*[46]

The Samaritan woman understands that Jesus' request is highly unusual for two reasons. In that time and culture, men did not speak to women who were not relatives. Even more, Jews did not associate with Samaritans. The woman responds with something like, "How can you ask me for a drink? Where do you get off talking to me. I don't know you. We're not relatives. And you're a Jew, I'm a Samaritan; we have nothing to do with each other."

Jesus' reply presses His invitation and hints at His identity, *"If you knew the gift of God and who it is that asks you for a drink, you would have asked him and he would have given you living water."*[47]

Either the woman didn't understand Jesus, or she knowingly avoided His answer and launched into practical and religious arguments. Again Jesus invites her to ask Him for living water to drink. He says to her, *"Everyone who drinks this water will be thirsty again, but whoever drinks the water I give him will never thirst. Indeed, the water I give him will become in him a spring of water welling*

---

46   John 4:7
47   John 4:10

up to eternal life."[48] Jesus says this to a broken woman who had been married to five husbands and was currently living with a man who was not her husband. This behavior caused her to be an outcast.

Twice she dismisses Jesus' invitations by changing the subject with arguments, but Jesus is persistent, ultimately declaring to her, *"I who speak to you am he."*[49] Jesus is reaching back to Moses' conversation with God in the burning bush. Moses, too, had met every invitation from God with an excuse or objection.

Moses said to God, *"Suppose I go to the Israelites and say to them, 'The God of your fathers has sent me to you,' and they ask me, 'What is his name?' Then what shall I tell them?"*[50]

God responded to Moses, *"I am who I am." This is what you are to say to the Israelites: 'I am has sent me to you.'"*[51]

The Samaritan woman acknowledges to Jesus that she believes the promise of the Messiah and that when He comes everything will be explained. Jesus responds, *"I who speak to you am he."*[52] Jesus is the living water who eternally quenches our thirst. Jesus is the great *I am*. He is both the one who invites, and He is the invitation.

When the disciples returned from town with food they were surprised to find Jesus talking with the woman. She accepted Jesus invitation, left her water jar, returned to town, and told her neighbors, *"Come see a man who told*

48   John 4:13-14
49   John 4:26
50   Exodus 3:13
51   Exodus 3:14
52   John 4:36

me everything I ever did. Could this be the Christ?" They came out of the town and made their way toward him.[53]

As a result of her brief encounter with Jesus, the Samaritan woman's life was transformed. *"He told me everything I ever did."* The woman, who once was a village outcast, drawing water alone at the well in the sixth hour because of her sins, had become an evangelist for the Christ. *Many of the Samaritans from that town believed in him because of the woman's testimony.*[54]

Jesus persisted in offering Himself, the Living Water, the *"I am,"* to the Samaritan woman. He saw her broken and wounded heart and addressed her deep need. She in turn made an invitation to the town's people of Sychar that brought many to faith. Jesus' encounter with the Samaritan woman became a mission of salvation and peace to a people long rejected by Israel.

The third example comes from the last chapter of Luke. In it Cleopas and an unnamed friend, discouraged and confused, are walking from Jerusalem on the road to Emmaus. The crucifixion of Jesus had destroyed their hope that He was the long promised Messiah. Their confusion arose when the women who had gone to Jesus' tomb came back and told the disciples that the tomb was empty. They said an angel had told them that Jesus was risen.

As the two disciples walked along, a third man overheard their conversation and inquired, "What are you discussing?"

---

53   John 4:29-30
54   John 4:39

Cleopas responded, "Haven't you heard what happened to Jesus in Jerusalem?"

"What?" the man inquired.

As they walked toward Emmaus, Cleopas and his companion shared with the man all that had occurred in the Holy City during the past few days. The stranger's response to the news was direct. It led to a revelation and an invitation. He said to them, *"How foolish you are, and slow of heart to believe all the prophets have spoken!"*[55] Beginning with Moses, He explained to them all that the Scriptures reveal concerning the Christ.

As they approached a village, the man appeared to be going farther, but the disciples invited Him to share their lodging and dinner. At dinner the man took bread, gave thanks, broke the loaf and gave it to them. At that moment their eyes were opened, and they recognized the stranger as the risen Jesus. He immediately vanished. In the action of breaking the bread, Jesus made Himself known and invited them to receive Him. Jesus is the invitation. Cleopas and his friend quickly returned to Jerusalem to tell the eleven disciples that they, too, had seen the risen Christ.

We are a lot like these two disciples. For a brief moment they saw the risen Lord. Their eyes were opened; their discouragement, doubt and confusion were erased. But after Jesus vanished, they had to *"live by faith and not by sight."*[56] Like Cleopas and his friend, we struggle with waves of doubt and confusion, but in celebrating the Lord's Supper we, too, know His presence in the breaking of bread.

---

55   Luke 24:25
56   2 Corinthians 5:7

Jesus is the invitation. A life surrendered to Him and filled with His promised Holy Spirit enables a believer to make the invitations He made. Jesus' promise is that from those invitations His church will do even greater things than He did.[57] That is the ministry and mission of His followers who are the Church. Accepting and making Jesus' invitations begins in worship.

---

57   John 14:12

PART III

WORSHIP

THE PURPOSE OF WORSHIP

WORSHIP IS THE VEHICLE by which the omnipotent Triune God connects with His creation. It is a key way that God reveals Himself to humanity. The apostle Paul tells us that God *"…is before all things, and in him all things hold together."*[58] The Old and New Testaments reveal that God is above and beyond everyone and everything. We worship Him because He is the Creator of all things, especially us; the Giver of all life, particularly ours; the Savior of all sinners, you and me; and the Master of all human destiny. In worship our reasoning, pride, and achievements, no matter how great, are humbled in the radiance of His transforming presence.

He is a God of relationships, even in His very being: Father, Son and Holy Spirit. In worship we learn to surrender ourselves – body, soul and spirit – to God. He desires that we worship Him corporately in spirit and truth.[59] Friendship with God is the most important bond we ever make. Like any important relationship, it takes an investment of time and effort. We are to relate to each other in the same way. Although we begin with an individual response to God's invitation to Jesus as Savior and Lord, we are not intended to come to Christian maturity alone. In

---

58   Colossians 1:17
59   John 4:23-24

Romans, the apostle Paul says, *". . . so in Christ we, though many, form one body, and each member belongs to all the others."* [60] In 1 Corinthians, he says, *"The eye cannot say to the hand, 'I don't need you!' And the head cannot say to the feet, 'I don't need you!'"* [61] Worship is God's way for us to develop an intimate friendship with Him and with Christian sisters and brothers. Those friendships are deepened through worship. It is where we embrace His purpose for our life, joining with others to grow in maturity and become His royal priesthood and holy nation. Like stones in a rock tumbler, we spend a long time knocking off the rough edges and polishing one another. This is the process of sanctification that matures our character, revealing God's presence in us. Worship is intended to glorify God and change us for the better.

There are many different forms of Christian worship. It can take the form of daily tasks or a leisurely walk in the woods, but for the purpose of this book, worship is what happens in church on Sunday morning. Normally, Christians think of growing in Christ as an ongoing process that happens during their day-to-day lives while studying the Bible, through private devotions, or in fellowship, but not during an hour of worship on Sunday morning. Eugene Peterson has long been one of my at-a-distance role models for pastoral care and preaching. His understanding of worship is very deep. He maintains that worshiping God in Christ is the most important and difficult thing that Christians do, affecting heaven and earth. Yet, in his many books, he has repeatedly asserted that nothing

---

60   Romans 12:5
61   1 Corinthians 12:21

much happens during Sunday morning worship, and as for preaching, we've pretty much heard it all before.[62] I don't think he is being facetious. Perhaps this sad situation has come about because we view ourselves as pursuing God and have become weary of the effort. Scriptural accounts of Jesus' invitations reveal that God is pursuing us much more intensely than we are seeking Him.

In contrast to today's typical worship service, "stuff " happened in Jesus' gatherings. People came to faith, the sick were healed of debilitating diseases, the dead were brought back to life, demons were cast out, and sins were forgiven. People were changed! Jesus promised His followers (who today are you and me), *"Very truly I tell you, whoever believes in me will do the works I have been doing, and they will do even greater things than these, because I am going to the Father."*[63] Jesus' "stuff" and greater things should be occurring in Christian worship today.

Jesus did not assemble an order of service for His followers to use when they worshiped. Instead He lived and taught the essential elements of a God-centered life. He did this by being the Lord of the Sabbath,[64] fulfilling Holy Scripture,[65] praying and teaching His followers how to pray,[66] giving sermons, teachings and parables,[67] forgiving

---

62   **Reversed Thunder**, Eugene Peterson, pages 142 & 146
63   John 14:12
64   Matthew 12:28, Mark 2:28 & Luke 6:25 *The Son of Man is the Lord of the Sabbath.*
65   Mark 4:4, 7 & 19 Jesus answers Satan's temptations in the wilderness with Scripture quotes. Jesus Christ is the New Covenant fulfillment of the Old Covenant.
66   Matthew 6, Mark 6:46, Luke 5:16 & John 17
67   Matthew 5-7 - Sermon on the Mount

sins,[68] sharing the Lord's Supper with His followers,[69] and offering Himself on the Cross.[70] Subsequently, the Church organized these elements into an order of worship that has evolved over centuries. Today, the sermon has become a predominant element of worship for both the protestant and sacramental branches of the Church. Missing today is the glue that held all the elements together for Jesus – invitations.

THE SERMON AND INTERACTIVE WORSHIP

Why do people come to church? I don't think people showing up on Sunday morning are looking for more *information* about God. They want to *experience* Him. Many church services today are one-dimensional with no interaction. Worship manuals often script the order of a Sunday service. Clergy or lay leaders offer prayers with little opportunity for the congregation to make their own petitions and thanksgivings to the Lord. The usual worship format could be described with a theater analogy: the pastor, assistants, and music leaders are the actors; the congregation is the audience. God provides the script through Holy Scripture and the order of worship. Essentially, the audience is only eyes and ears, seeing and hearing what is presented. There is little opportunity for people to respond to the script.

68   Matthew 26:28 & Acts 2:38
69   Lord's Supper - Matthew26:26-27, Mark 14:22-23, Luke 22:19 & 24:30
70   Crucifixion John 19:15-37; Matthew 27:33-44; Mark 15:22-32; Luke 23:23-26, 44-47

Invitations are not made, and God who is present is not expected to act.

Invitational interactive worship is a two way street that facilitates spiritual growth. To make the theater analogy interactive, imagine the worship service with this format: everybody is an actor, including God who provides the script that is taken from Holy Scripture and the order of worship. With this configuration some actors (predominantly the clergy) offer invitations, others respond. The congregation speaks to God in prayers, praises, and responses; God acts and speaks to them, addressing their needs and maturing them as they worship. The epistle to the Hebrews tells us, *"For by one sacrifice he has made perfect forever those who are being made holy. The Holy Spirit also testifies to us about this. First he says: 'This is the covenant I will make with them after that time, says the Lord. I will put my laws in their hearts, and I will write them on their minds.'"*[71] God intends that people will be changed in their minds and hearts by worshiping Him.

Frequently, Christian worship is focused on acquiring information through preaching that involves only listening. Holy Scripture is read, expounded upon, and summarized with a pastoral prayer. This worship pattern could be called the 'sermon dynamic.' In this type of worship there is no interaction. The preacher makes compelling points, leaving the listeners to process later what they have heard. "Good sermon," mumbled over an extended hand at the door gives the preacher an immediate grade, but congregants rarely remember the main points of the sermon by

---

71   Hebrews 12:14-16

lunchtime, let alone during the remainder of the week. If they haven't absorbed the message, they will not be changed. In order for people to assimilate the content of the sermon, they need some way to interact with the material before leaving church. An invitation taken from the Scripture readings and sermon offers that opportunity.

The information offered in worship is intended to become knowledge, but knowledge is only part of the equation. Experience has a much more lasting effect than only hearing. People are more likely to talk about things they have actually experienced. The person who is healed is enthusiastic about sharing what has happened and who was responsible for it.

A leper reached out to Jesus and begged to be made clean. Social norms did not allow interaction with lepers, who were considered spiritually unclean. Jesus accepted the man's impassioned plea. Touching the man, Jesus said, *"I am willing. Be clean!"* [72] Immediately leprosy left the man. Jesus sent the healed leper away with a strict warning not to tell anyone, but to show himself to the priest and offer sacrifices of thanksgiving. Instead the man began to talk freely, spreading his good news. [73]

The man's joy overwhelmed Jesus' request for silence. The Samaritan woman's encounter with Jesus caused her to become the village evangelist. Like the leper and the Samaritan woman, when we experience a manifestation of God's grace, we are willing to share the wonder of it with anyone who will listen. We are less inclined to share insights gained from only hearing a sermon. A witness of

---

72   Matthew 8:3
73   Mark 1:40-45

faith comes from our heart, not just our head. God-authored experiences in life and worship are the "stuff" of our witness that touches the heart of another.

St. Mark's, Shelby, was a parish of deep faith. For the many decades of its history, dedicated clergy had taught the fundamentals of Holy Scripture and the intricacies of the denomination. With all that knowledge, there was an underlying realization by the entire membership "that there must be something more." We were seeking the other part of the equation, the experience. In groups of four or five we piled into cars and traveled to other churches where we had been told exciting worship was happening. In these congregations, St. Mark's parishioners heard invitations for repentance, healing prayer, and blessing. The experience of responding enabled the knowledge in our heads to become reality in our lives.

In order for worship to be effective, knowledge must be married to experience. Experience is what brings knowledge alive. We need both. In church the glue that joins knowledge and experience is invitations. An invitation based on a sermon, teaching, or prayer allows people to immediately respond to what God is doing in their hearts.

In some churches the sermon is often followed by an invitation to come forward and receive Jesus. During several waves of the Great Awakening, powerful preaching in widespread revivals led to a profound sense of conviction and repentance on the part of people who responded to what became known as the 'altar call.' The altar call is most often associated with an invitation to make a personal first time or reaffirmed decision for Christ, accepting Him as both Savior and Lord. In protestant churches this addresses the spiritual need for salvation. In sacramental churches, the Lord's Supper issues a similar invitation, "Come and receive Jesus."

The Lord's Supper and the Altar Call have traditionally been the only invitations offered in Christian worship. But Jesus surrounded the salvation invitation with other invitations that addressed the needs of people. Jesus' invitations drew people to Him, but also interactively connected people - those who came for healing, those who brought them, and those who watched.

What if all forms of Christian worship today contained the kind of interactive invitations that Jesus issued? Perhaps people would be drawn to the church's worship. Today the Church is dwindling in membership. Invitations to "experience" the Lord are generally not made either inside or outside of worship. In a culture that has become increasingly hostile to Christianity, now is precisely when the heartfelt faith of individual Christians and the Church needs to be seen and heard.

Story: Giving My First Worship Invitation

For all the sermons I'd preached, I hadn't seen much change in parishioners' lives. In preparing my sermons I relied on Scripture and hearing the Lord, but sometimes, even while I was preaching, the Holy Spirit completely changed the sermon. Frustrated, I asked, "Father, if You're that concerned about the content of the sermon, why aren't You concerned about the way listeners process it?"

"I am," He spoke into my spirit. "Douglas, you must make an invitation in the worship. Listen to Me."

Obviously, I hadn't been doing *my* part. God didn't nudge me; He shoved me in the direction of making an invitation based on the Scripture lessons and content of my sermon. The goal was to address people's needs, while connecting the congregation with God and each other.

At St. Mark's on a Sunday morning in mid-Lent, instead of a sermon, I shared my experience of receiving Jesus at the revival service in the Bay Village shopping mall.. My expectations were low. In spite of doubts and significant anxiety, I issued this invitation, "I've never done this before. Honestly, I'm really nervous. If you've never made a conscious decision to accept Jesus as your personal Savior and Lord… if you've never surrendered all your life to Christ… or if you did that a long time ago and need to do it again… I invite you to get out of your pew and join me at the altar rail so we can pray together."

There were forty-eight people in church that morning. Over half the congregation came forward to join me for prayer, many with tears running down their cheeks — more tears of joy than sorrow. This was the altar call part of the invitation. It was followed by the interactive part. Family and friends stood behind those who had come forward and placed their hands on shoulders while I prayed. After the prayer, hugs were shared all round. It was a Sunday recorded in our hearts, and I'm sure noted in Heaven. That day marked a significant step forward in St. Mark's long history of faithfulness in Shelby and beyond.

FOUR ESSENTIAL ELEMENTS OF INVITATIONAL INTERACTIVE WORSHIP

Through the experience of issuing my first worship invitation, I came to realize that I didn't understand the basic elements of invitations. Knowing and incorporating those elements would facilitate interactive worship that brings people together with the Lord and each other.

In the New Testament there is a pattern of four essential elements in Jesus' invitations: obedience, hospitality, proclamation, and ministry. Jesus washing the feet of His disciples at the Last Supper illustrates how these elements work together in worship.

In obedience to the Law, Jesus instructed His disciples to make preparations for the Passover.[74] He practiced hospitality by hosting the Passover meal. He proclaimed the New Covenant He was instituting[75] and ministered to His disciple's by washing their feet.

Jesus' actions during the supper are an example of humble obedience. *Jesus knew that the Father had put all things under his power, and that he had come from God and was returning to God; so he got up from the meal, took off his outer clothing, and wrapped a towel around his waist.*[76] The Apostle Paul is blunt: Jesus is doing the task of a slave.[77] Jesus is being obedient to His heavenly Father's prompting.

After that, he poured water into a basin and began to wash his disciples' feet, drying them with the towel that was

---

74   Luke 22:11
75   Luke 22:20
76   John 13:3-4
77   Philippians 2:7, **The Message**

wrapped around him. "No," said Peter, "you shall never wash my feet."

Jesus answered, "Unless I wash you, you have no part with me."

"Then, Lord," Simon Peter replied, "not just my feet but my hands and my head as well!" [78] Peter's first response to Jesus is disobedience. Jesus' response to Peter and the other disciples is a proclamation in the form of an implied invitation. *"Those who have had a bath need only to wash their feet; their whole body is clean. And you are clean, though not every one of you."* [79]

Washing feet was part of Jesus' ministry to His disciples at the Last Supper. It was carried out with love and humility. His ministry was an expression of deep friendship and strong encouragement for all they were about to experience in His crucifixion. It is a model for all servant-hearted ministry.

Jesus' proclamation continues: *When he had finished washing their feet, he put on his clothes and returned to his place. "Do you understand what I have done for you?" he asked them. "You call me 'Teacher' and 'Lord,' and rightly so, for that is what I am. Now that I, your Lord and Teacher, have washed your feet, you also should wash one another's feet. I have set you an example that you should do as I have done for you.* [80]

Obedience, hospitality, proclamation, and ministry are as relevant for worship today as they were at the Last Supper with Jesus.

---

78   John 3:5-9
79   John 3:10
80   John 13:12-15

1. OBEDIENCE

First and foremost in invitational worship, church leadership must hear and be obedient to the Holy Spirit's promptings before, during, and after services. From Genesis to Revelation, the Bible has much to say about obedience. When God gave the Ten Commandments to Moses and the Hebrew people, He began with this instruction: *So love God, your God; guard well his rules and regulations; obey his commandments for the rest of time.*[81]

In the New Testament we learn through the example of Jesus Christ that believers are called to a life of obedience. The concept of obedience in both the Old and New Testaments is submitting to God's authority. In order to submit to God's authority, we need know and understand Holy Scripture and hear His 'voice.' We hear God's voice in different ways at different times. It may be during private devotions or corporate worship. For me, it's always when I am quiet and listening. God most often speaks to me through Holy Scripture. Sometimes He may use mental pictures and impressions, or as Leonard Sweet says, 'nudges.'[82] Occasionally His voice to me is even audible. With practice and in time, His voice becomes recognizable over all the other voices that clamor for attention. Hearing God's voice and following His direction is essential, though it's not always easy. Leading invitational interactive worship is not a technique; it is a relationship with God.

---

81   Deuteronomy 11:1 The Message
82   **Nudges: Awakening Each Other to God Who's Already There** by Leonard Sweet.

As a small boy, Samuel was brought to the Temple by his mother to serve under the priest, Eli. In those days God's voice was rarely heard by anyone. Eli had gone to bed. Samuel lay down near the Holy of Holies where the ark of God was housed. Then the Lord called to Samuel. Thinking it was Eli, Samuel answered, *"Here I am, you called me."*

This happened three times. Then Eli realized that the Lord was calling the boy. So Eli told Samuel, "Go and lie down, and if he calls you, say, 'Speak, Lord, for your servant is listening.'" So Samuel went and lay down in his place.

The Lord came and stood there, calling as at the other times, "Samuel! Samuel!"

Then Samuel said, "Speak, for your servant is listening."

Initially, Samuel did not recognize the Lord's voice, but over time, he came to know when the Lord was speaking to him. *The Lord was with Samuel as he grew up, and He let none of Samuel's words fall to the ground.*[83] Israel acknowledged Samuel as a prophet. God revealed Himself to Samuel through His Word. Like Samuel, you and I must learn to recognize and be attentive to God's voice.

Story: Immediate Obedience

The day had been long, beginning with early morning meetings, working on Sunday's bulletin, and the monthly newsletter. The afternoon was devoted to pastoral counseling appointments. The time between the appointments was salted with telephone calls and peppered with drop-ins; a mixture of people looking for a handout and parishioners and friends who dropped by to say, "Hello."

---

83   1 Samuel 3:1-19

The parish secretary, Laura, left the office at 5:30, leaving me alone with a male counselee. An hour later I locked up the offices and headed home. Taking a short cut through residential neighborhoods, I passed Barney and Marge Taber's home. They had started attending St. Mark's seven months ago after moving into the area from Detroit. "Douglas, stop at the Taber's house now," the Lord said clearly.

Barney worked the second shift at Shelby Sales Book, leaving Marge home by herself. "Lord, it's been a long and exhausting day. I'm tired and late for dinner. I'll see Barney and Marge later in the week. I promise."

At the stop sign at the end of the block, He spoke again. "Douglas, turn around and go back to the Taber's house immediately."

"It's late. Barney's at work. Marge will be alone. I don't do house calls on women alone. It's a wise principle that You taught me. I'll see them tomorrow." A hint of irritation had crept into my response.

In the center of the next block, the Lord spoke a third time, "Douglas, now!"

Angrily, I pulled into a driveway to turn around and head back to the Taber's, remembering the counsel of a seminary professor: "Doug, if you find a portion of Scripture where God repeats Himself, pay careful attention and purpose to be obedient." This wasn't Scripture, but it certainly qualified as repetition.

On the front porch, I knocked at the door several times without a response. Marge probably isn't even home, I thought impatiently. As I was about to leave, Marge opened the door dressed in faded jeans and a powder blue sweatshirt that identified her as "Grammy." Although it was a warm spring day, she wore a heavy, full-length terrycloth robe over her outfit, triggering a red flag in me. Marge looked distressed. She had been crying, as evidenced by the puffiness under her eyes and the wadded Kleenex in her hand.

"Father Doug, I was praying to Jesus to send someone to help me," she blurted with a mixture of surprise and relief, "I've been so depressed. Barney and I had a horrible argument just before he left for work." She began to cry again, wiping her eyes and nose on the sleeve of her robe. "I took all my anti-depressant medication to kill myself and punish Barney. When I realized what I'd done, I laid down on the bed. That's when I began to ask Jesus for help. 'If You don't want me to die, please send someone to help me....'"

"Everything will be all right, Marge," I assured her. I opened the screen door and pushed past her toward the phone in the hall to call 911. "Tammy, this is Fr. Doug, please send an ambulance to the Taber's. Marge took an overdose of anti-depressants about forty minutes ago." I turned to Marge, "How many pills did you take?"

"I just got the prescription filled. Maybe twenty-five or thirty."

"Her speech is beginning to slur, and she's having trouble staying awake."

"We'll be there immediately." Moments later I heard the siren. Marge had collapsed on the living room couch still in tears and fighting sleep. I sat down beside her and took her hand.

"They'll be here soon."

"I don't want to die," she said, struggling to speak. "You're the answer to my prayer."

While the ambulance was on its way, I prayed with Marge. Then trying to keep her awake, I explained how I'd come to be on her doorstep. "You've taught me the importance of immediate obedience," I shared as the paramedics prepared to take her to Shelby Memorial Hospital. By God's grace Marge made a full recovery, and the Taber's marriage was healed.

2. HOSPITALITY

The early church understood the critical importance of hospitality. The apostle Paul makes special note of the hospitality extended to him by Publius, who came to the aid of all who were shipwrecked with Paul on the island of Malta.[84] In Paul's letter to the Christians in Rome, he names with gratitude the people who have assisted him in carrying the mission of Christ forward. Paul thanks Gaius for extending to him and the church in Rome hospitality that was enjoyable.[85] Hospitality is so important to church life and the spread of the Gospel that Paul encourages the Roman Christians to practice hospitality for it is love in action. *"Love must be sincere. Hate what is evil; cling to what is good. Be devoted to one another in love. Honor one another above yourselves. Never be lacking in zeal, but keep your spiritual fervor, serving the Lord. Be joyful in hope, patient in affliction, faithful in prayer. Share with the Lord's people who are in need. Practice hospitality."*[86]

---

84   Acts 28:7
85   Romans 16:23
86   Romans 12:9-13

Hospitality is seeing another person as Jesus sees them and treating them as He would. One Sabbath Jesus was teaching in a synagogue. He saw a woman who for eighteen years had been bent over and crippled by an evil spirit. *When Jesus saw her, he called her forward and said to her, "Woman, you are set free from your infirmity." Then he put his hands on her, and immediately she straightened up and praised God.*[87] The synagogue leader was indignant because, in his understanding, Jesus had broken the Sabbath law. From Jesus' perspective hospitality and compassion were consistent with the intent of the Sabbath observance. *"The Sabbath was made for man, not man for the Sabbath."*[88]

In church, Christian hospitality is more than coffee hour, potlucks, prayer breakfasts, or even home fellowships. As the church, we are called to welcome guests, help those in need, and do good deeds.[89] The absence of invitations in Christian worship lessens the opportunity to invite newcomers into the transforming presence of God where they can be encouraged to accept Christ as their Savior and grow in faith. Invitations address worshipers personal needs and deepen intimacy with their heavenly Father and the Body of Christ. In addition, invitations provide opportunities for maturing believers to practice ministering to others. It is as simple as asking, "How can I pray for you?" or holding a hand.

---

87   Luke 13:12-13
88   Mark 2:27
89   1 Timothy 5:10

Story: A Miracle for Brenda

Brenda Harris had been attending St. Mark's for a little more than a year. She had been warmly welcomed and soon became a member of the congregation. Her presence required careful attention and extra effort on everyone's part. Brenda suffered from seizures, some violent; with others she simply fell asleep. As a teenager, she had been in an automobile accident and sustained a major head trauma. A hand-sized portion of her skull had been crushed and replaced with a stainless steel plate that doctors believed was now causing the seizures. The electrical impulses of Brenda's brain were somehow short-circuited by the metal plate in her head.

Unable to drive, Brenda walked to church. As a result of seizures suffered at church, parishioners watched her closely. At a Wednesday night prayer and praise meeting, I made an invitation for anyone in need to receive prayer. Brenda shared her need and asked for healing prayer. Several of us laid hands on her and anointed her head with Holy Oil from a Cruet. The oil ran through her hair and dripped from her chin. Brenda began to laugh with the joy of the Lord.

Three months later Brenda came to my office and showed me a sharp bump that had appeared on her scalp. She feared that the metal plate was breaking loose. I prayed for Brenda again and urged her to immediately see her physician. A week later, Brenda reported, "My doctor can't believe what's happened. The Lord has grown new skull bone beneath the plate. It's pushing the plate up. I'm going to the hospital in a few days to have it removed. But best of all, I haven't had any more seizures. God is so good!"

I agreed and prayed in thanksgiving for answered prayer, successful surgery, and an effective witness to her surgeon. Brenda was completely healed and a year later was issued a license to drive. The hospitality of the Body of Christ had welcomed and surrounded a newcomer with acceptance, love and watchful prayer.

Story: Are We a Friendly Church?

A year into Christ the King's life as an independent congregation we began to ask ourselves if we were a "friendly" church. The answer given by parishioners was a resounding, "Yes, of course we are. We're very friendly."

I countered, "I agree. We are friendly with one another, the people we know. Let's spend the next few weeks asking visitors what they think. Are we welcoming? Are we hospitable? Are we as friendly as we think we are?"

The result of our month long inquiry of visitors, particularly at Sunday morning worship, was truly disturbing. No, we weren't welcoming, hospitable or friendly to the stranger in our midst. We got along famously with the people we knew, but not so much with the people who were visiting.

In response to that startling revelation, the parish leadership devoted several weeks to repentance and confession, not only asking forgiveness for our inhospitality, but also petitioning the Lord for a way forward. The parish leadership met after Sunday worship for several months to role-play identifying and greeting visitors, seeing to their comfort, and answering questions. It was our goal to introduce visitors to several parishioners and at least one of the clergy on their first visit. After worship, visitors were invited for refreshments that had been moved from the Fellowship Hall to the more accessible Narthex at the entrance of the church. If a friendship was forming, the leadership was encouraged to invite new people to coffee or lunch. In addition, the bulletin contained a statement of welcome and ways visitors could connect with the church. To make participation more accessible, the order of worship was projected on overhead screens.

The realization of our inhospitality brought about significant changes. Change is always difficult. The Lord's conviction reordered parish priorities consistent with Jesus' Great Commandment[90] and Great Commission.[91] Jesus taught about hospitality in the context of calling His followers to practice servant-hearted character. We are to *"be salt of the earth"* and the *"light of the world."*[92] How do we become salt and light? Jesus promises His followers the Holy Spirit. *"If you love me, keep my commands. And I will ask the Father, and he will give you another advocate to help you and be with you forever— the Spirit of truth. The world cannot accept him, because it neither sees him nor knows him. But you know him, for he lives with you and will be in you."*[93]

---

90   John 13:34-35
91   Matthew 28:18-20
92   Matthew 5:13-14
93   John 14:15-17

With the guidance of the Holy Spirit we are able to make invitations that draw people to Jesus. Invitations aren't complicated. They can be as simple as:

"Please, sit here with me."

"Let's have coffee together. I'll treat."

"You sound really distressed. How can I pray for you?"

"How about coming over for dinner on Friday. Bring your kids."

"Before you go, would you let me pray for you?"

Hospitality changed the environment of Christ the King Church. Our experience in determining whether we were a friendly church was reminiscent of the cartoon character Pogo Possum's statement, "We have met the enemy… and he is us." [94] Unless a church is hospitable, the kingdom of God cannot be advanced. We at Christ the King Church began to live what we believed and proclaimed.

3. PROCLAMATION

The proclamation of the Holy Scripture is a prelude to issuing invitations in the hospitable environment of interactive worship. Eugene Petersen paraphrases the apostle Paul's words about the necessity of proclamation, *"But how can people call for help if they don't know who to trust? And how can they know who to trust if they haven't heard of the One who can be trusted? And how can they hear if nobody tells them? And how is anyone going to tell them, unless someone is sent to do it?"* [95]

---

94   Wait Kelly's cartoon character Pogo Possum to Albert Alligator
95   Romans 10:14-15a, **The Message**

I had been treating my congregation solely like an ear. Paul used a humorous, yet convicting analogy, *"If the whole body were an eye, where would the sense of hearing be? If the whole body were an ear, where would the sense of smell be?"* [96] Ideally Sunday worship should involve all the senses and speak to the whole person – body, soul and spirit. Jesus spoke to the whole person; so should we.

Jesus' presence, teachings, and parables were launching points for invitations that welcomed people to receive ministry from Him. At the feeding of the five thousand, Jesus invited those who had followed Him from Nazareth to share a miraculously multiplied meal.[97] Later, at the feeding of the four thousand, Jesus went up on a mountain where great crowds had gathered to hear Him speak. His message was welcoming and at the same time convicting. People responded by bringing to Jesus *"the lame, the blind, the crippled, the mute and many others."* [98] The people who followed Jesus onto the mountain had been away from their homes for three days. Jesus knew they were hungry. After proclaiming the Good News, He offered hospitality by miraculously providing abundant food for them.[99]

The Gospels and Book of Acts repeatedly record Jesus' pattern of gathering people to hear the Good News followed by an invitation that allowed them to respond to what they had heard and seen. The invitations resulted in ministry that manifested itself in conviction, repentance,

---

96   1 Corinthians 12:17
97   Matthew 14:13-21
98   Matthew 15:30
99   Matthew 15:29-39

salvation, healing, signs and wonders, even deliverance and resurrections.

Those Scriptures caused me to wonder, how I could implement invitations in worship? The Holy Spirit led me to open my Bible to Peter's first recorded sermon delivered on the day of Pentecost. Those who had received the Holy Spirit as Jesus had promised were in the streets speaking in other tongues. The crowd that gathered was comprised of Jews from every nation. They were bewildered because each one heard the Good News from Jesus' followers in their own language. Some people mocked the disciples and accused them of being drunk. Had I been there, I might have done the same. Peter addressed the crowd with a bold, convicting invitation that began with, *"God has made this Jesus, whom you crucified, both Lord and Messiah."* [100]

Ouch! That's a withering accusation. The street crowd on Pentecost had been pierced to the heart by Peter's words. Not being constrained by polite church culture, they demanded, *"Brothers, what shall we do?"* [101]

An invitation unfolded in Peter's response, *"Repent and be baptized, every one of you, in the name of Jesus Christ for the forgiveness of your sins. And you will receive the gift of the Holy Spirit. The promise is for you and your children and for all who are far off—for all whom the Lord our God will call."*

With many other words he warned them; and he pleaded with them, "Save yourselves from this corrupt generation." [102]

---

100   Acts 2:36
101   Acts 2:27
102   Acts 2:38-40

Peter counseled the crowd to repent and be baptized. This is a crucial invitation. Luke tells us that more than three thousand people responded positively. They accepted Peter's invitation and were baptized as a sign of their faith.

I read these passages with new eyes. The simplicity and bluntness of the invitations was striking.

Story: Forgiving Brings Forgiveness

At Christ the King Church, the first sermon I preached with an invitation began as a proclamation from the Lord's Prayer. I started with, "God loves us extravagantly and unconditionally, we don't have to do anything to earn His love, but you remember that within the Lord's Prayer, Jesus emphasized that there is a condition on our receiving the Father's forgiveness. To be forgiven we must forgive. Jesus said, *'For if you forgive other people when they sin against you, your heavenly Father will also forgive you. But if you do not forgive others their sins, your Father will not forgive your sins.'* [103] This is more about the person forgiving than the person being forgiven."

My intent was to explore this truth as an intellectual exercise. Forgiveness frees a person of anger, resentment, unforgiveness, and bitterness. Forgiveness heals a broken heart. This is a huge need. As I approached the conclusion, the Holy Spirit interrupted, "Douglas, you have touched a place of pain in the hearts of many people. Invite them to come forward for prayer."

---

103   Matthew 6:14-15

Since I, too, was struggling with anger and forgiveness, I said to the Lord, "Why would I willingly open myself to another person's pain? I have enough of my own."

"It's also the beginning of a blessing," the Lord assured me.

Here was the essence of my invitation, "If you are harboring unforgiveness in your heart toward someone… perhaps it's a recent offense… possibly it's something that was said, done, or left undone by a person long ago… they may even be deceased… come forward to the altar rail. By coming forward you are acknowledging that you have made a decision to completely forgive the person for whom you've been harboring resentment… and perhaps a desire to get even…." Before I could finish, over half the congregation had walked forward, about seventy people. I was stunned. God's word goes forth and does not return empty!

"Yes," I continued, "it's about releasing that person, but even more it's about God forgiving, healing, and releasing you. Father God loves you and honors your forgiveness." Collecting my wits, I immediately sought the Lord and awkwardly assured God's forgiveness to those who had risked coming forward. I prayed aloud that the Lord would heal wounds in body, soul and spirit. The tears in my eyes mirrored the tears in the eyes of many parishioners. Forgiveness had set us free.

4. PRAYER MINISTRY

We most often practice prayer as a conversation with God in which we talk and He listens. But it is much more important that we listen to God. Wherever two or three are gathered for prayer in Jesus' name, He is present.[104] It is in His presence that the needs of people are addressed. Listening is essential in prayer ministry. We need to listen to both the person's need and the Lord's direction. When appropriate, offer an invitation, "Would you allow me to pray for you right now?" Pray and do what the Holy Spirit instructs. Stay calm and go slowly.

Prayer ministry may be witnessing a person's commitment, new or renewed, to Jesus Christ.[105] It may involve hearing a person's repentant confession of sin and assuring the person of God's forgiveness.[106] Often it is listening to a person's need for physical, situational or relational healing and responding with prayer. Sometimes it even involves deliverance. Approximately one third of Jesus' ministry entailed deliverance.[107]

Ministering in prayer is not for the purpose of counseling, advising, or "fixing" the person. To do so is to risk wounding by conveying judgment. The goal of prayer ministry is for the recipient to be firmly rooted in the love and victory of Jesus Christ. If a physical healing occurs, it is important that the prayer ministers strongly encourage the recipient to have the physical healing confirmed by a physician.

Jesus prayed authoritative, simple prayers. The attitude of the heart of the person praying is more important than eloquence. I believe prayer ministry teams should consist of both a man and woman for the comfort of the recipient

---

104   Matthew 18:20
105   Mark 16:16
106   Matthew 6:12-14
107   Luke 7:21

and for a balanced gender perspective. They should pray in a unity of spirit with their eyes open in order to be attentive to body language. With the recipient's permission, they may place their hands on the person's head or shoulders.[108] The team may also anoint with Holy Oil[109] in the sign of the Cross. In the event the Holy Spirit overcomes the person, be prepared to gently lower him into a chair or to the floor. Someone should sit with the person so that spiritual rest is not interrupted.

Prayer ministry often addresses deeply personal issues. Most people are cautious about being vulnerable. Therefore, the church should be a safe place. Confidentiality is essential. People presenting themselves for prayer must know that their privacy will be honored. If an extreme pastoral concern emerges, the person should be urged to seek further ministry from the clergy.[110ψ]

Paul calls us to identify with the sufferings of Christ. He also promises that we will share in Christ's glory. To be open to God and present oneself for prayer ministry is to be spiritually enlarged. To minister in prayer is to empathize with the struggles of others. This is the basis of our interdependence in the Body of Christ. When we remain isolated from one another we are incomplete. In isolation we may be joined to the head, Jesus Christ, but we are missing the other body parts. Being prayed for and praying for others connects us in the Body. It is in the church that our

---

108   Luke 4:40
109   James 5:13-16
110   ψ People who reveal that they are contemplating suicide must be reported to clergy and the proper authorities.

brokenness is mended, and our wounds are healed. It is where we mature and are equipped for ministry.

Story: Coffee Shop Prayers

I was having coffee with a guy who had become a friend and parishioner. The cups were almost empty and the conversation was winding down. We'd shared some intimate matters with one another in our time together. I asked, "Sam, how can I pray for you?"

He was quiet. While considering what to share, he finished his coffee. Haltingly he began, " I have a brother who lives with his family in Wyoming. We don't see each other much any more. They have a dog, Rex, who is a treasured pet. Rex is old and dying. I guess you could pray for him and my brother's family."

In our conversation, Sam had shared intense struggles about his job, the challenges of prostate problems, and the troubles he and his wife were having raising two rebellious teenagers; but when offered an invitation to prayer, he distanced himself. I realized that my question had raised intimacy issues. Rather than address his obvious needs, Sam requested prayer for his brother's old dog in Wyoming. He was hoping that, at best, I'd put his request on my prayer list or just forget it.

"Sam, that's a situation that needs some prayer, but we've discussed a lot of deep concerns. Jesus is here with us. He loves you and invites you to share your needs. How can I pray for you right now, out loud, and face to face?

"You'd do that?"

"Yes."

Sam ran his hand through his hair and groaned, "Ok… I'm exhausted… maybe a little depressed… and I'm afraid of losing my job."

Reaching across the table, I placed my hand on Sam's. He closed his eyes, but I kept mine open and prayed a brief prayer, asking the Holy Spirit to renew his strength and to help him secure his employment.

I ended the prayer, "Amen."

Sam opened his eyes, wet with tears, and whispered, "Thanks."

Story: A Sacrifice of Prayer for Doris

"The Body of Christ, the bread of heaven."

"Amen."

"The Blood of Christ, the cup of salvation."

"Amen."

Holy Communion had been distributed, thanksgiving offered, and the final blessing given. Before the recessional hymn, I regularly invited anyone who needed prayer to come forward to the altar rail where I would pray with them. Everyone had gradually made his or her way to the undercroft to partake in coffee, the liquid that lubricates Christian fellowship. The altar rail was empty.

My wife, Eleanor, helped me hang up my vestments so that I wouldn't get in trouble with the Altar Guild who bustled about quietly with their duties. Turning from the closet, I looked out the sacristy door. Doris had come forward to the altar rail and knelt down, obviously distraught. I went inside the altar rail to kneel in front of her. Eleanor stood behind her with her hands on her shoulders. With a trembling voice Doris said, "I found a lump on my breast a few days ago. I have an appointment with a surgeon tomorrow. They think I need a mastectomy." She began to sob.

As Doris knelt for prayer, Zorayda ceased her duties in the sacristy and made her way to the last pew. Not given to emotion, Zorayda had held the innovations I recently introduced at arms' length. She knelt in the back and slowly lifted her arms in prayer.

"Doris, would you place your hand over the lump?" I asked. Placing my hands gently on her head. I prayed, "Lord Jesus, thank You for being Doris' great physician. Thank You that You have promised that it is by Your stripes that Doris is healed. We thank You for removing every cancerous cell from her body, not only her breast, but anywhere that rebellious cells have metastasized. Doris, I speak into your body, soul, and spirit the peace and healing of Jesus that passes all understanding."

I anointed Doris' forehead with Holy Oil, marking her with the sign of the Cross. Together we said, "Amen."

Zorayda was still kneeling in the last pew with her arms raised. I knew that she suffered from arthritis in every joint. She had been holding her arms up for over ten minutes. Excruciating pain was etched in her face. She had offered her pain as a sacrifice of love and an act of intercession for her sister in Christ. The next day, the surgeon was unable to find the lump in Doris' breast. The surgery was canceled.

Story: "Not yet, Pauline."

On a sizzling California Sunday, every church window was open and all the fans had been drafted into service in a futile attempt to cool the sanctuary. Wilted worshippers unenthusiastically intoned *"How Great Thou Art"* as the offering was received. Mid-stanza, Pauline, an elderly parishioner, meticulously dressed in her "Sunday best," collapsed in her pew in the center of the congregation. Parishioners near Pauline heard the death rattle escape from her throat before she slid to the floor. Kathy, a cardiac nurse at Santa Clara Hospital, rushed to Pauline's side to check her pulse. Kathy's head appeared above the pew. Looking directly at me, she mouthed, "Pauline's dead."

Signaling the musicians to be silent, I instructed an usher to call 911 and immediately invited the congregation to pray. We petitioned the Lord to breathe life into Pauline and heal whatever had caused her to collapse. Kathy disappeared between the pews to begin CPR. The spiritual tug of war for Pauline's life was tangible as we interceded for what seemed like an eternity. Suddenly Kathy's head popped back up. "She's alive! Praise God, she's back with us." The congregation broke into applause and choruses of praise.

Pauline stood, struggling for balance while straightening her outfit. "What happened?" she inquired, obviously disoriented.

"It looked like you were on your way home to Jesus," I explained.

"That's what I thought. It looked like Heaven, and I wanted to stay, but He said, 'It's not your time yet, Pauline.' So here I am," she said with a hint of irritation.

Two Campbell medics burst through the door with a gurney in tow. They attempted to get Pauline to lie down, but she refused, "I'm fine really. Let's go back to worship."

"No, you're coming with us," they insisted.

Still refusing help, Pauline was escorted to the ambulance by the medics who firmly insisted that she have a thorough check-up at a hospital.

"Was she really dead?" I asked Kathy after the service.

"Yes, very much so. She didn't have a pulse, and I hadn't started CPR when the Lord brought her back."

"That's a miracle! Thank you, Lord," I said with profound gratitude.

Kathy nodded enthusiastically in agreement, "Yes! Yes it is!"

Pauline's death and return to life had demanded that the congregation respond to an urgent need. The Lord had gotten our attention. It was a lesson that shaped the future of the congregation.

Story: Prayer - Eyes Open and Out Loud

Lindsey and Brad had received Holy Communion. Grasping her husband's hand, Lindsey walked with determination to the blessing station where Eleanor and I offered prayer at the contemporary service of First Presbyterian Church, Ambler. She smiled, pulling her husband up close. "We want to pray for Emily and Kevin."

"Yes definitely," we agreed. Emily and Lindsey were friends. Emily attended the Bible Study that Eleanor and I led. She had invited Lindsey, a young wife and mother, to join the fellowship.

Emily's fiancé, Kevin, had been rushed to the emergency room twice within a week, but the diagnosis remained uncertain. Lindsey and Brad held hands. Eleanor placed her hand on Brad's shoulder, and I placed mine on Lindsey's as we interceded for friends in a time of crisis.

One of the disciplines that I've taught prayer teams is to pray with eyes open. Most people pray with eyes closed — except while driving. Lindsey's eyes were closed. Her brow was creased with determination. Brad, whom we had only met briefly, stood rigid with his eyes open. He looked uncomfortable.

Praying with eyes open allows prayer team members to see the body language of the people for whom they are praying. They also have to be alert to expressed needs and the Holy Spirit's direction. As we ended our petitions for Judy and Paul, the Lord directed me to pray for Lindsey and Brad, "Lord bless this marriage. Grant Lindsey and Brad a deep unity of spirit in their relationship with one another as husband and wife, and as the parents of Jacob and Andrew. Thank you Lord for their sons, and the enormous blessing they are to this family. Help Lindsey and Brad raise their sons to be all that You have created them to be and to walk in every good work You've prepared for them."

Lindsey let out a sigh of approval and squeezed her husband's hand in a non-verbal, "Amen." Brad look surprised. I took out my Oil Stock and anointed both of their heads with Holy Oil in the sign of the Cross, "Lord Jesus, increase Lindsey and Brad's love for one another."

All four of us agreed saying, "Amen."

"Thank you, we didn't expect that," Lindsey offered. "We truly need it." Brad nodded in agreement as a smile began to light up his face.

Story: Message for John

Arms outstretched, spread as wide apart as possible, grinning from ear to ear, John headed straight for the prayer station with a throaty laugh. Hugging both of us, he announced, "I need prayer."

For several months John's knees had been bothering him. Not enough to keep him off the Pocono Mountain ski slopes, but enough to cause pain and produce a noticeable limp that temporarily erased his engaging smile.

Eleanor and I hugged him back. "Brother John, we will pray for you," I declared, matching his smile and planting my hand on the top of his head. "Lord, you haven't healed John's knee, but You are certainly enlarging his heart. He limps with the joy of Your love and victory.

"John, in the mighty name of Jesus Christ your Savior and Lord, we bind you to the things of God: His Word in Holy Scripture, the Cross of Jesus where your victory is secured, and the gifts and fruit of the Holy Spirit who lives in you. In Jesus' name we loose you from the world, the flesh – especially the weakness in your knees – and the devil. God loves you abundantly. You are secure in Him."

Jesus Christ gives us the authority to "bind" and "lose" as a strategy to address sin in the world. *Truly I tell you, whatever you bind on earth will be bound in heaven, and whatever you loose on earth will be loosed in heaven.*[111] Binding and loosing are to be done with two or three in agreement. Eleanor and I were in agreement.

---

111   Mathew 18:18

"Yes, yes… amen!" John said with enthusiastic conviction, adding his affirmation to the unity of spirit.[112] I made the sign of the Cross on his forehead in Holy Oil. "Thank you, I needed that," he said, hurriedly leaving to minister to a brother who was returning to his pew from Communion.

Eleanor looked at me with a mixture of concern and surprise. "Is something wrong?" I asked.

"No, not at all. The Lord gave me a Scripture for John, but he's already gone."

"Do you want me to find him?"

"No. I'll just write him a note," Eleanor assured me.

Here's what she wrote to John: "My spiritual connection must be on dial-up because I didn't get this word until after you left the prayer station Sunday. So here it is slow, but still true: *The prayer of a righteous man is powerful and effective.*[113] John, I don't know the prayers of your heart, but I do know that you are a righteous man. I trust that as you persevere in prayer, the Lord is bringing the answers. God bless you."

Eleanor listened. The Holy Spirit authored her response and the note. The next Sunday, John told us that he was encouraged and blessed.

NOT JUST IN CHURCH

The previous stories were all in the context of Sunday morning worship, but Jesus' ministry was primarily in the world. During my retirement in Pittsburgh, I was a

112   Matthew 18:15-19
113   James 5:16

deckhand on RiverQuest's environmental education vessels. Minus a title and collar, I quickly came to realize that I now faced the same challenges of sharing my faith that all my parishioners had confronted daily.

As a deckhand I cared for the vessels and kept watch on the passengers to see that they were comfortable and, more importantly, safe. Passengers often started a conversation with a seemingly simple question. Once the question was answered, people sometimes shared very personal concerns. This surprised me since I was a complete stranger.

On one cruise an exhausted middle-aged woman grasped my arm, "How do I get upstairs?"

I directed her to the steps on the stern deck.

She thanked me, paused, and then threw up her hands in exasperation, "I don't know what to do. I think my daughter's on drugs."

Once a disheveled high school student sat down next to me on the stern bench, "I just don't get it. I think I'm failing. My parents will be devastated. I must be as stupid as my Dad says I am. What should I do?"

On another voyage, a rough, white bearded man who appeared to be a "biker" asked, "When's this damned thing over?"

"It'll be another half hour before we dock, " I replied.

Impatient, he let out a deep sigh, "My marriage is a wreck. I just don't know what to do. I think my wife's going to divorce me."

"Would you let me pray for you?" I asked.

The biker looked surprised, "I don't believe in that stuff. But I guess it would be OK. Sure, go ahead. It can't hurt."

In all these instances, I asked the Lord to help me see and hear the person with my own understanding and the insight of the Holy Spirit. My response to the person was to listen, and then ask, "Would you allow me to pray for you, right here, right now?" That is what I had learned from Bob and Zorayda, the ministry of prayer, face to face and out loud.

In three years as a deckhand, not once was I turned down in my offer to pray with people who shared needs. I never saw those folks again, but God knows who they are and loves them. He made the divine appointments. The great evangelist and prayer warrior, George Muller, once said, "We have a prayer hearing and answering Father." There are people all around you who are carrying unmet burdens and painful needs. In my flesh I would never have had the boldness to make those invitations, but with the guidance of the Holy Spirit, I was able to do it. So can you.

PART IV

BUILDING BLOCKS OF INVITATIONAL INTERACTIVE WORSHIP

CHANGE

CHANGE IS ALWAYS CHALLENGING. An example of change that has become accepted in worship services is the passing of the Peace. People look at a neighbor and say, "The peace of the Lord Jesus be with you." The response is, "And also with you." What began as an awkward handshake and reluctant verbal exchange of greeting has become a warm hug. Change requires perseverance for both the congregation and the leadership.

As a worship leader I struggled with many elements of the Sunday morning experience. One element always stood above the rest — TIME! In most churches, worship lasts an hour or at the very most, an hour and fifteen minutes. Invitations can take time away from other important parts of the order of worship. To be honest, there is always a person or two who watches the clock. Instead of a handshake and, "Good Sermon," they point to their wristwatch and admonish, "Pastor, you ran over again."

The Rev. Mike Flynn, founder and leader of Fresh Winds Ministries, Burbank, California, is a friend and mentor. After a long day of ministry at Christ the King, we were resting in my living room. I shared my concern about the impact invitations had on the time allotted for worship. I will never forget the wisdom that Mike shared: "God is the author of the _Book of Common Prayer_, and He's read your order of worship in the bulletin. Listen to the leading of the Holy Spirit. He understands and works within the time allotted. Doug, you don't have to do **everything** every Sunday." Mike's words lifted a heavy burden from my shoulders. In order to keep worship time reasonable, I realized it would be possible to eliminate parts of the service. I was never led to eliminate Holy Communion, but the number of Bible readings was at times reduced from four to one. Sometimes the Creed, Confession, or hymns were eliminated for a Sunday in order to accommodate those who had responded to an invitation. This juggling took practice!

After a time of experimenting with invitations in worship, I eventually learned that the bulk of prayer ministry was best accomplished after the final blessing. The Rev. Chuck Irish was the head of the Episcopal Church's Charismatic Movement. He used to say prior to the dismissal, "Now you have some options. You can stay for prayer and ministry. That's what I'll be doing right up here. You can go to the fellowship hall and have coffee with your brothers and sisters in Christ. Or maybe you need to go home. If you stay here, the people you came with will wait for you. Come or go in peace to love and serve the Lord Jesus Christ."

The Lord impressed upon my heart three additional insights that resulted in changes in the way I led worship. First, congregational worship must be a process of leadership functioning in unity to welcome people into God's presence. Second, the content of the Scripture readings should determine the theme for the entire worship experience: sermon, music, invitations and ministry. Third, as the pastor of a small congregation, I quickly came to understand that there are only so many times you can give an altar call to accept Jesus Christ as Savior and Lord. With one hundred or fewer people attending Sunday morning worship, a traditional altar call can begin to feel like judgment. The pastor knows, or should know, everyone. They all know the pastor, and probably have known each other for a long time. Too many altar calls in a small congregation can quickly turn into 'calling people out' – more like confrontation than loving invitation. Salvation wasn't the only invitation Jesus made, and the altar call shouldn't be the only invitation we make.

Changing from traditional patterns of worship to interactive worship requires patience and a willingness to risk making mistakes, but the effort produces much fruit.

TRUTH AND HONESTY

Truth and honesty undergird interactive worship. Jesus embraced both when He told the Jews who claimed to believe in Him, *"If you hold to my teaching, you are really my disciples. Then you will know the truth, and the truth will set you free."* [114] Jesus knew that they were not being honest or telling the truth. They were looking for a way to kill Him.[115] When Jesus revealed to His disciples that He would soon be put to death, they were frightened and perplexed, not understanding what was about to happen

---

114   John 8:31-32
115   John 8:37

or where their Lord was going. Jesus comforted them and comforts us when He said, *"I am the way and the truth and the life. No one comes to the Father except through me. If you really know me, you will know my Father as well. From now on, you do know him and have seen him."* [116] If Jesus Christ is the truth, then being less than truthful is moving away from Him. Being truthful and honest is about following in God's footsteps, for He does not lie. It is being more God-like, more God-centered. We need to be honest with Jesus, with ourselves, and with one another. *"Surely you desire truth in the inner parts; you teach me wisdom in the inmost place."* [117]

Story: A Child Will Lead Them

Our Savior Episcopal Church continued to grow, but the diocese increasingly marginalized the parish. Ultimately, the parish handed over its buildings and assets to the diocese. We became Christ the King Church, an independent congregation with an Anglican culture. With the help of the Campbell City Council, the congregation found a new home in a large industrial building only four blocks away.

Although we had quietly departed the denomination, diocesan hostility toward the parish continued. In the Apostle Paul's letter to Christians in Colossae, he instructs, *"Let the peace of Christ rule in your hearts, since, as members of one body, you were called to peace. And be thankful."* [118] We were drifting far afield from this core principle.

116   John 14:6-7
117   Psalm 51:6 **NIV Classic Reference Bible by Zondervan**
118   Colossians 3:15

During the Sunday children's sermon, following a week of very unpleasant interactions with the diocese, the Associate Pastor, Larry McMinn, asked the children, "What do we do that makes Jesus sad?"

It was an invitation soliciting a response. One child volunteered, "Disobey my parents."

Another ventured, "Not telling the truth."

Then seven-year-old Kaleo spoke out clearly, "Falling into the world."

There was a gasp from multiple people in the congregation, then the sound of people getting on their knees... followed by silence. It was a profound word from God spoken by a child: Scriptural,[119] brief, true, and convicting! The contentiousness of our relationship with the diocese and the denomination was consuming us like the dynamic of a dysfunctional family. All we knew of church life was conflict; we were losing sight of Jesus. Our relationship with the diocese was causing us to fall into worldly behavior. We were beginning to forget that our struggles are not against people, but against spiritual forces of evil.[120] Kaleo's word reminded us that we are to function according to God's principles, not the world's. It was an invitation to let go of the conflict, enter peace, and join Jesus in His kingdom mission. Sometimes an invitation is for the congregation as a whole. Over a decade later, parishioners still remembered God's Word spoken to us from the lips of a child.

---

119   Isaiah 11:6
120   Ephesians 6:12

Story: We're All Lost Sheep

The Fourth Sunday in Lent was one of those days for which Californian's apologize. Morning fog had struggled to clear, revealing high clouds that blocked the sun. The overcast weather seemed to reflect the mood of the people gathering for worship. A life sized wooden Cross, already covered with notes containing confessions of sin stood ready to receive more. The Gospel reading was the Parable of the Lost Sheep.[121] Before a mixed crowd of the curious and hostile, Jesus reveals that He is the Good Shepherd, who leaves the ninety-nine in search of the one that is lost. My message had a strong evangelical theme that appeared to be going well when the Holy Spirit interrupted me, "Everyone here is saved. Trust Me, I know. Invite those who are saved, but still feel lost, to come forward."

"Right now?" I questioned in silence.

"Right now," He responded in a gentle, but firm command.

"I haven't finished…" I whined.

"Douglas…."

My fumbling about must have looked like I'd lost my place in the sermon notes. I looked up to a congregation that was watching me with anticipation.

"Be honest," the Holy Spirit urged.

Running my fingers through my hair, I began, "Everyone here at one time was lost, but Jesus Christ found you, and brought you home to Father God with great rejoicing. Jeff and Paula have often told us in song that 'life is hard and it might not get easier.' In the midst of life's hard

---

121   Luke 15:1-7

challenges some of you may have come to feel like you are lost again. I know… I've experienced that, too. Four years into ministry, I found myself angry with God, frustrated and floundering. I was lost and looking for a way out." Choked with emotion, my voice began to fall.

Remembering my mother's admonition to speak up, I raised my head and increased my volume, "Your heavenly Father loves you extravagantly. He created you with a purpose and plan for your life. Jesus Christ is now and always will be your Good Shepherd. The Holy Spirit lives in you. He is your compass to keep you in the way, the truth and the life. If you're feeling lost, I invite you to come forward to the altar step right now…."

Nothing happened. No one budged. I'd learned to be patient and wait, looking and listening. There were sniffles and a few sobs. People were reaching for the Kleenex boxes at the end of each row. Then Earl stood, his hands covering his face. He stumbled over several people to reach the center isle. Coming forward he exclaimed, "Pastor Doug, I'm a mess."

Gradually people stood and joined Earl at the front of the church. People came forward in tears, two and three deep at the altar step, and behind them ministry teams stood with their hands extended in prayer for hurting friends. I prayed a general prayer for all who had responded to the invitation, and encouraged them and the prayer teams to remain as long as needed. Heeding Mike Flynn's wise counsel, we set aside the Creed, Confession, Intercessions, and Offertory (yes, that, too) and moved to Holy Communion, which was distributed at stations, allowing the ministry to continue at the altar step. People stayed after the final hymn. The praise band and vocalists remained, offering songs of worship until everyone was finished with prayer and ministry.

After coffee and fellowship, I fell on my knees before the Cross in gratitude for God's direction and the abundant healings, victories and blessing that He had manifest that cloudy morning. I made a mental note to get more Kleenex. As I locked the church doors, I noticed that the sun was shining.

RELEASING LEADERSHIP

There have been seasons when the cry of my heart took on the sour note heard in Moses' grumbling. Moses railed at God for the burden of leading the stubborn Israelites through the wilderness. God heard his complaint. Moses said, *"If this is how you are going to treat me, please go ahead and kill me – if I have found favor in your eyes – do not let me face my own ruin."* [122]

I was about to lock-up the church and head home for Sunday lunch, totally exhausted from the demands of leading worship. Weekly teachings (I rarely preached) had been followed by invitations for which almost the entire congregation came forward for prayer. After worship, waves of people sought me out for counseling. I was done in and about to complain to the Lord. He spoke succinctly before I got a chance, repeating what He had said before, "Douglas, equip my saints for the work of service." It was a reminder once again to give away the ministry He had entrusted to

---

122   Numbers 11:15

me. The Lord never intended that I do this alone; it's the ministry of the whole Body of Christ.

One aspect of leadership is the ability of the leader to effectively delegate authority. Moses' father-in law, Jethro, saw that Moses was wearing himself out as the lone leader. He encouraged Moses to *"select capable men from all the people—men who fear God, trustworthy men who hate dishonest gain—and appoint them as officials over thousands, hundreds, fifties and tens.... That will make your load lighter, because they will share it with you. If you do this and God so commands, you will be able to stand the strain, and all these people will go home satisfied."* [123]

When Moses took this concern to God, He said to Moses: *"Bring me seventy of Israel's elders who are known to you as leaders and officials among the people. Have them come to the tent of meeting, that they may stand there with you. I will come down and speak with you there, and I will take some of the power of the Spirit that is on you and put it on them. They will share the burden of the people with you so that you will not have to carry it alone."* [124]

In the church today when people complain that their needs aren't being met, the frequent response by leadership is to add staff. However, if the church tries to meet needs without mentoring lay leadership, the paid staff may increase, but ministry will not multiply. It is the responsibility of the leadership to nurture the gifts and fruit of the Holy Spirit in church membership. They must give away what they've been given in order for ministry to expand.

---

123   Exodus 18:21-23
124   Numbers 11:16-17

It's what Jesus did with His twelve disciples, and later His seventy-two followers.

In the New Testament, Jesus sent out His twelve disciples with power and authority to drive out demons, cure diseases, heal the sick and proclaim the kingdom of God.[125] Later, under the demands of increasing crowds and intensified opposition from religious rulers, Jesus appointed seventy-two followers and sent them out in pairs ahead of Him to the places He was about to go.[126] They prepared the way of the Lord.

When the disciples couldn't meet the needs of the growing church in Jerusalem, the Twelve gathered all the disciples and chose seven to help them oversee the distribution of food so they could focus on prayer and the ministry of the Word.[127] This pleased the whole group and stopped the complaining. *They presented these men to the apostles, who prayed and laid their hands on them. So the word of God spread. The number of disciples in Jerusalem increased rapidly, and a large number of priests became obedient to the faith.*[128]

Moses, Jesus and the twelve disciples took the ministry entrusted to them and gave it to followers who showed evidence that they had reached a level of maturity and preparedness for new and greater responsibilities. God the Father poured out the Holy Spirit upon leaders and prophets in the Old Testament and believers in Christ in the New

---

125   Luke 9:1-2
126   Luke 10:1 & 17
127   Acts 6:1-7
128   Acts 6:6-7

Testament. As a result of the followers' ministry, Jesus said He saw "*Satan fall like lightening....* "[129]

It took several years to implement a church environment that encouraged parishioners to practice using the gifts of the Holy Spirit with one another in church before going out into the world. Our primary mission field is where we live: family, neighborhood, recreation, school, and job. God also places on the hearts of some individuals and congregations opportunities for outreach to other parts of the world. Whether at home or in a far away mission, Christians all share the responsibility of being God's witnesses.

---

129   Luke 10:18

PART V

RESULTS OF USING THE SCRIPTS

IMPLEMENTATION OF INVITATIONAL INTERACTIVE WORSHIP

THE DEVELOPMENT OF THE SCRIPTS for The Tabernacle and The Ten Gates expanded our understanding of how to issue many different kinds of invitations during worship. As a result, our worship also became much more interactive. Like a new pair of glasses that brings clarity to vision, invitational interactive worship helped us recover our focus on Jesus Christ. He had gradually become out of focus in the press of the world, the pursuits of the flesh, and the distractions of the devil. Eugene Petersen writes: "The work of worship gathers everything in our common lives that has been dispersed by sin and brings it to attention before God; at the same time it gathers everything in God's revelation that has been forgotten in our distracted hurrying and puts it before us so that we can offer it up in praise and obedience." [130]

By God's grace, over the years my focus cleared, and the way I led worship changed. I stopped opening services with prayers that invited Jesus into our midst. He is already present. Instead I boldly proclaimed, "Jesus is here!" I repeated this until I heard an equally energetic response, "Jesus *is* here!" Then I declared, "We're in God's transforming

---

130 **Reversed Thunder: *The Revelation of John and the Praying Imagination,*** Page 189

presence. Let's be attentive to God: Father, Son and Holy Spirit. Let's be joyful and expectant in our worship." The business card for Christ the King Church held this statement under the parish name: "Where Jesus faithfully meets us." I share this with you because whether clergy or laity, in worship you are welcoming people into God's presence.

Invitations can be made throughout worship. At the beginning, it's important to address people's immediate concerns so that they are not distracted. They are then free to hear the Lord about deeper needs for themselves and others. After the greeting I frequently said, "If you had a difficult week... a problem at work... a disturbing visit with your doctor... or trouble getting to church this morning... maybe the kids dallied, or you and your spouse found yourself at cross-purposes... if so, please raise your hand. If you don't have your hand up, please move next to someone who does and place your hand on their shoulder while I pray for us." The "Amen" was often followed by quiet laughter indicating that the invitation had struck a chord.

The Lord urged me to offer many different forms of invitations in worship. Initially the invitations came from our Anglican culture as a sacramental congregation. Within that culture, there were already places around the worship space where people could stop and reflect: the Stations of the Cross, stained glass windows, and a columbarium. Often people were seen touching a niche to give thanks for a loved one now at home with the Lord.

The traditional places of reflection lead to more interactive opportunities where people could gather in response to invitations. During Lent there was a life-sized wooden

Cross at the front of the sanctuary. People were encouraged to write their confessions on red slips of paper that they nailed to the Cross. This could happen at anytime during worship, which meant that the sound of hammering a nail might accompany the sermon. At Good Friday's worship, the pieces of paper were taken down and burned in the parking lot. The flames were the outward sign of the inward grace of God's forgiveness.

From Pentecost to Advent, a large lighthouse replaced the wooden Cross. Parishioners were urged to join with Christians from churches across the Santa Clara Valley to become lighthouses of prayer by praying for their neighbors. During worship people could put the first names of their neighbors, the address of their neighborhood, and prayer concerns inside the lighthouse. The following week I included those petitions in my prayers.

Throughout the church year the Baptismal Font, filled with Holy Water, stood at the entrance to the church. People could touch their forehead with a wet finger or make the sign of the Cross and reaffirm their baptismal promises. We borrowed the idea of Votive Candles from our Roman Catholic brothers and sisters and placed them at both the front and back of the church. Lighting a candle is an act of faith that God hears and answers our prayers.

From Easter Sunday to Pentecost, there was a tableau depicting the rolled away stone and empty tomb of Jesus Christ where worshippers could celebrate His resurrection. An open area at the back of the church allowed people to stand, kneel, lie prostrate or dance if so moved.

At the weekly celebration of the Lord's Supper, I invited the congregation to stretch forth their hands and join in the prayer of blessing over the bread and wine. We are all God's *"chosen people, a royal priesthood, a holy nation, God's special possession...."*[131]

During and after Holy Communion, the Altar Rail became the location for prayer ministry teams, as well as a place for people to respond to the invitations made during the sermon and liturgy. Prayer teams were also attentive to people remaining in the pews who needed prayer. Holy Oil was available in Oil Stocks near the Communion Table for anointing.

The stories shared earlier tell of the personal and corporate changes the Lord authored as together we put Jesus first, listened to Holy Scripture, and followed the leading of the Holy Spirit. Yes, we made mistakes, but in God's mercy He redeemed them. He taught us valuable lessons. By implementing them, we blessed many people and glorified God.

A lesson that I learned when I first began to issue invitations during worship was the importance of being precise and clear with both the invitation and ways of responding. A vague invitation can be challenging to the leadership, confusing to the congregation, and embarrassing to the respondents. One of my mistakes followed the Gospel reading of Jesus blessing infants and children.[132] My invitation welcomed parents and children to the altar rail for prayer to be blessed and be a blessing to one another. Unfortunately, I neglected to say when this should happen. As a result some families responded immediately, some seemed confused, others waited until after Holy Communion.

131   1 Peter 2:9
132   Luke 18:15-17

Everyone was a bit embarrassed. If I had been clear about the timing of the response and ministry, I would have spared us the discomfort. Clarity is an important element of issuing invitations.

Some of the opportunities for invitations should have been obvious, but it took me awhile to see them. In the United States there are four national holidays that address individual and shared needs: Mother's Day and Father's Day – the responsibility of parenting; Veteran's Day – the duty, honor, and sacrifice of military service; and Labor Day – the necessity of and commitment to work. At the Sunday worship closest to the holiday, I invited the people being honored to the altar step for prayer and a blessing. Often family members and friends stood behind them placing their hands on their shoulders in support of their service and sacrifice. What parent, veteran, or laborer doesn't need prayer?

All invitations depend upon the leadership listening to the Holy Spirit, being obedient to His promptings, and stepping out in faith. God is the author of the invitations; the pastor is the messenger. Making invitations in the midst of worship may seem complicated and a little risky. If so, the following is a basic invitation that I made at the conclusion of every worship service, "If you came here today with a concern or need that hasn't been addressed in prayer, please come and kneel at the altar step. There will be people here to pray with you. I'll be here, too. If you came with family or friends, be assured that they will wait for you. You are welcome here in the presence of the Lord Jesus who loves you. Please don't go home without your concerns being addressed in prayer." The altar step at the conclusion of worship never stood empty. Some members brought family and friends to church specifically for the prayer ministry at the altar rail.

UNITY, FRIENDSHIP, HOLINESS

The **Tabernacle** and **Ten Gates** scripts were transformational in the life of Christ the King Church, but we soon discovered that their impact was more far reaching. They facilitated three fundamentals that are essential to healthy church life and advancing God's Kingdom: unity, friendship, and holiness. Sharing the scripts with neighboring congregations helped bring unity to the church in the city. Standing, praying and serving together built friendships across denominational lines. It also matured Christian character, which is an important part of holiness. Unity, friendship and holiness grew the priesthood of all believers in San Jose. Most believers were called to be witnesses in their own neighborhood, but the Lord called some into ordained ministry; others became short and long-term missionaries sent from the city to far away places. The good fruit born of our surrender to God's will – unity, friendship, and holiness – surprised us, grew the whole church, and blessed the city.

Unity

Unity, although difficult to achieve, is essential both within a congregation and among churches in a city or region. Cities are no longer surrounded by protective walls and guarded by gates to manage the entrance and exit of traffic. Today human and technological institutions provide protection. Urban centers have swallowed up small towns and become megalopolises. These vast mission fields are in desperate need of the Good News.

History tells the story of the Church fracturing over doctrinal differences, territorial disputes, and conflicts between government and church leaders. This was particularly true during and after the Reformation. Church factions figuratively dismantled the wilderness Tabernacle and carried off pieces that often became the focus of their identity. Some churches have several pieces of the Tabernacle, others have fewer, but no one church possesses everything. The Baptists have the laver; the Orthodox have the veil; the Roman Catholics have the altar of incense, etc. And yes, there are some churches that want nothing to do with any of it.

The megalopolis of Silicon Valley was the home of more than six hundred Christian congregations. Pray South Bay was an ecumenical organization in the valley that sought unity. Approximately seventy clergy from churches micro to mega gathered monthly to pray under the leadership of Pastor John Isaacs. We were a remnant. While the Silicon Valley had experienced explosive growth, the church as a whole had begun to decline. The Pray South Bay pastors did a demographic study and determined that for the church to stay even with population growth, we would need two hundred new congregations, each with 150 to 250 members. Due to tax revenue issues, the city had enacted legislation declaring, "No new churches!"

A number of Pray South Bay pastors were present at a presentation of **The Tabernacle:** *God's Portrait of Jesus Christ*. Afterward, we realized that each of us had been entrusted with stewardship over a portion of the Tabernacle. When we brought those pieces together in unity, as Jesus prayed we would, astounding things occurred. Jesus prayed, *"I pray also for those who will believe in me through their message, that all of them may be one, Father, just as you are in me and I am in you. May they also be in us so that the world may believe that you have sent me. I have given them the glory that you gave me, that they may be one as we are one—I in them and you in me—so that they may be brought to complete unity."* [133]

Over a period of twenty years this diverse, competitive and, at times, combative gathering of Christian leaders eventually learned to stand, pray and serve together. That is our work; God's work is to build His Church. Our first inclination was to try to do God's work because we found it more exciting than the humble tasks He had assigned us. And yes, when we attempted to do God's work, we failed, wrapped in the sins of pride and competitiveness.

As the Pray South Bay clergy yielded to the labor and sacrifice of becoming one, God healed the longstanding hostile relationship between the Church and the city of San Jose. The Lord brought us into a deeper unity than we had ever imagined possible. During the decade of the 90's, San Jose became the safest city in United States. A large Christian school was granted land and building permits to establish a new middle and high school on premium land

---

133   John 17:20-22

within the county. San Jose's City Counsel repealed the "no new churches" legislation. God sovereignly, over the course of two decades, added more than two hundred new congregations, most with their own building, to the Church in Silicon Valley.

Together the Church's witness is powerful; fragmented the Church's witness is tarnished and diminished. Only together can we fulfill our Lord's Great Commission. Only together serving in unity can we bring the Good News into and out from today's cities.

Friendship

Where did the two hundred new congregations in the hostile Silicon Valley come from? They were the sweet fruit of Christian friendships that crossed denominational and congregational boundaries. They were the answered prayers and good works of neighborhood missionaries who stood, prayed and served together in the places where they lived. Having identified the gifts God had entrusted to them, believers were able to stand at the spiritual gates of their neighborhood and minister God's grace.

The Pray South Bay pastors discovered that their members did not know their immediate neighbors regardless of their race, culture, or language. The people in the homes to the right, left, and across the street were complete strangers. They didn't know their names or what occupied their time and energy. Children weren't let loose to play in neighborhoods after school, instead they were engaged in organized activities or pre-arranged play dates. The pastors acknowledged that this was a painful reality for them as well. We were clueless about our own neighborhoods. We were residents, not neighbors or friends.

This realization brought about the birth of a movement called Lighthouses of Prayer. Every Christian in San Jose was challenged to see their neighborhood as their primary mission field. Initially parishioners prayed for ten to thirty houses, condominiums, or apartments around them. This proved to be too much. The strategy was revised: "Step out your front door and pray for the homes you can see from there. Pray for and bless your neighbors. Ask God to orchestrate meaningful encounters, building a neighborhood filled with friendships."

It only takes one Christian to be the catalyst for a neighborhood. On my street, I was not that person. Tom, my Roman Catholic neighbor was the relationship glue who held the neighborhood together. He was friendly and encouraging as witnessed by the story in which Tom and I prayed for Alden. Making neighborhood friendships opens the door for sharing faith. This can and must happen everywhere Christians are found. Not every believer is called to be a missionary in some far away place. However, every Christian is called to be a missionary in their community, standing as a friend at the gate of their neighborhood, praying for their neighbors and even strangers as they come and go.

Holiness

At the conclusion of **The Tabernacle: *God's Portrait of Jesus,*** I always invited people to sit in the Holy of Holies on the Mercy Seat beneath the wings of the Cherubim. Many people accepted that invitation. They sat quietly, often with tears in their eyes. Many told me that looking out from the Mercy Seat, they came to see what God sees – our broken-ness and the gift of His amazing grace. This new awareness moved them to be more loving. *"Be holy because I, the Lord your God, am holy."* [134]

Holiness is to love God and others in thought, word and deed, as Jesus loves us. The apostle Paul writes, *"Love is patient, love is kind. It does not envy, it does not boast, it is not proud. It does not dishonor others, it is not self-seeking, it is not easily angered, it keeps no record of wrongs. Love does not delight in evil but rejoices with the truth. It always protects, always trusts, always hopes, always perseveres. Love never fails."* [135] To be holy is to love like Jesus loved.

Jesus' love was experienced in the invitations He made. Likewise, our love is often expressed through invitations. In the absence of love, invitations are infrequently offered. Without love, friendships are conditional, unity is tenta-tive, and holiness is impossible. Human love infused with God's extravagant love builds friendships and forms unity that nurtures holiness within believers and the church. The apostle Paul says it succinctly; *"The only thing that counts is faith expressing itself through love... The entire law is*

---

134   Leviticus 19:2
135   1 Corinthians 13:4-7

summed up in a single command: 'Love your neighbor as yourself.'" [136]

The good news of the Gospel is that Father God loves us. His only son, Jesus, loves us so much that He was willing to die to pay the debt of our sins. God the Holy Spirit, out of love, has humbled Himself and made us His temple. God's love has set us free to live in victory that we might *walk in the way of love, just as Christ loved us and gave himself up for us as a fragrant offering and sacrifice to God.* [137]

Being loved by God and our brothers and sisters in Christ enables us to grow in our ability to selflessly love family, friends, neighbors and even strangers. Love builds friendships. Love grows unity within the family and the church. Love's sweet fruit is holiness.

A ROYAL PRIESTHOOD

The purpose of invitational interactive worship is to bring God's people into their new identity as a royal priesthood. In the Tabernacle we discover that every believer in Jesus Christ becomes a member of the tribe of Levi. The Levites were responsible for every aspect of the Tabernacle and later the Temple, including the priesthood. In Jesus Christ all followers become a holy nation and a royal priesthood. In the Tabernacle of the wilderness, we find a portrait of Jesus, a picture of us, a pattern of worship, and the promise of the Holy Spirit.

---

136   Galatians 5:6 &14
137   Ephesians 5:2

In the holy city of Jerusalem, the wilderness Taberna-cle became the Temple. The city's ten gates reveal both the gifts and the ministries God entrusts to us as His royal priesthood for building His kingdom. The Spirit nurtures the fruit of Christ-like character and gives gifts for doing what Jesus did and even greater things. It is essential that we know and put our faith in God: Father, Son and Holy Spirit. It is also essential that we know who we are in Jesus Christ and the gifts He has entrusted to us so that *"he who began a good work in you will carry it on to completion until the day of Christ Jesus."*[138]

When worship is invitational and interactive, God's equipping of His people to be a royal priesthood is facili-tated. People come to church on Sunday morning longing to experience God. They trust that He will meet their deep-est needs and answer the prayers of their hearts. In His transforming presence we begin the process of becoming servant-hearted representatives who bring blessing to oth-ers and glory to God.

God's love is revealed through believers like Bob and Zorayda in the hospital, and Elsie in her vision of a prom-ised future for a struggling congregation. We experience God's love through hospitality like Randall experienced at the parking lot picnic. We know God's love through prayer for a neighbor: like Alden's healing, Doris and Brenda's miracles, and Pauline being brought back to life. God's love is manifest in the blessing of Lindsey and Brad's mar-riage and parenting, Eleanor's note of encouragement to John, and Kaleo's word from God spoken in the midst of

---

138   Philippians 1:6

worship. The convicting lesson for the Brotherhood of the Golden Sword and the Oakmeal Fellowship was to surrender our life to Jesus Christ, to rest and laugh, to be honest and accountable. All of these experiences of God's love are the result of invitations made and accepted.

Jesus made invitations and commissioned His followers to do the same. Even more, Jesus Christ is the invitation. Love was in Jesus' warm smile from a picture hanging on Kim's bedroom wall. This love met her need, healed her broken heart, and gave her a future filled with hope. Jesus' inviting smile changed her life.

Invitations provide heavenly moments that transform lives, making ordinary people holy. Worship is the experience of entering the Holy of Holies through the Veil torn open by the hand of God so that we can sit on the Seat of Mercy beside Jesus. It is the place where we begin to see ourselves as He sees us and see what He sees. With this perspective, we are ready to explore the Gates and the Tabernacle.

THE SCRIPTS

INTRODUCTION

THE SCRIPTS of The Ten Gates of Nehemiah's Jerusalem and The Tabernacle: *God's Portrait of Jesus Christ* are an important part of the "how" of establishing invitational interactive worship within the life of a congregation. A general teaching on the subject would be non-interactive, whereas the scripts enable the congregation to experience and practice the concept. They solidify commitments to the Lord while furthering the process of Christian maturity and deepening fellowship. The invitations, responses, and resulting ministry strengthen the church and glorify God.

The scripts were developed at Christ the King Church in response to the following needs:

(1) to understand the connection between the Old and New Testaments

(2) to know the gifts God had entrusted to us individually and as acongregation

(3) to practice responding to invitations

(4) to learn how to offer prayer ministry in response to shared needs.

The Ten Gates of Nehemiah's Jerusalem enables people to identify the gifts the Lord has entrusted to them and the ministries to which they have been called. An added benefit is that respondents discover brothers and sisters who share the same gifts and ministry passions. The script contains an abundance of invitations that welcome responses and offer opportunities for prayer ministry. Ideally, it is presented on Sunday with the whole congregation. The experience should be filled with affirmation, laughter, and fellowship. This script made a significant contribution to Christ the King becoming a "friendly" church.

The Tabernacle: *God's Portrait of Jesus Christ* addresses making the connection between the Testaments and our faith today. It is full of invitations that offer opportunities to experience God's presence. People responding to invitations are welcome to receive prayer ministry from teams according to their needs. Twenty years of presenting **The Tabernacle** have proved the experience to be deeply spiritual and transformational for both the participants and those leading its presentation.

The scripts are yours to use as the Lord leads. Please remember that I am an Anglican. My denominational orientation is obvious, but not necessary to the effectiveness of these presentations. The scripts may be adapted as needs and resources require. The liturgy portions are from the 1979 <u>Book of Common Prayer</u>, but you can use forms that are part of your tradition. Some power point materials are included. You may wish to expand the content, adding artwork and music. Presentations have been made to both large groups with all that is suggested and to small groups as a bare bones version. Both scripts can be presented in a setting as simple as a living room or as elaborate as a church worship space.

Perhaps you are not in a position or don't have the time to introduce the scripts to your fellowship or church. I, too,

PART VI: THE SCRIPTS

have been in that place and found that both scripts are a source of biblical understanding, personal insight, and spiritual strength when used as a devotional. The Tabernacle and Jerusalem's Gates belong to God. He will lead you.

THE TEN GATES OF NEHEMIAH'S JERUSALEM

Introduction

Spiritual inventories were a source of frustration and disappointment for the parishioners at Christ the King Church. Elders, vestry, ministry teams and home fellowships repeatedly subjected their members to these evaluative instruments. The goal was to discover a person's top two or three gifts in order to better serve as a part of the Body of Christ. When the questionnaires were tallied many parishioners looked dejected.

"What's the matter, Sally?"

"This thing says I'm supposed to be a Sunday school teacher, but I have trouble relating to children. I don't know. It doesn't seem like me."

Many people found the results to be discordant with their self-understanding. Other parishioners discovered that their assessment didn't correspond with the way brothers and sisters in Christ experienced them.

"Hey, Frank, how did your spiritual inventory turn out?" I inquired.

135

"Great! Just great!" he shared, waving the pages of the scored document over his head. "It says I'm a prophet. How about that!"

"Hmmm," I mused, thinking to myself - they killed those guys. "That's great Frank, I'm sure I'll be hearing from you," I responded with an awkward laugh.

Periodically, staff meetings were peppered with complaints that the inventory assessments were failing to accurately help people identify the gifts of the Holy Spirit in their lives. Eloise Martindale, the parish Administrative Assistant, was inspired with an idea based on the Book of Nehemiah. Rough drafts and rewrites produced an interactive script filled with invitations that encouraged participants to explore God's gifting in their life and engage with other parishioners who identified similar gifts. While **The Gates** is still a gifts inventory, even more, it is a relational experience that involves others, rather than just filling out a questionnaire alone.

The Bible tells us that the King of Persia granted Nehemiah's request to return to Jerusalem and rebuild the city's devastated walls and gates. With the help of the high priest, Eliashib, and Ezra a priest, Nehemiah restored the walls of Jerusalem and the worship of God according to the Law of Moses. The church today, like the walls of Jerusalem, needs rebuilding. The presentation we developed enables people to identify their gifts so they can assist in the rebuilding of the church. In the script the purpose of each gate is explained along with its application for Christians today. Following a gate's explanation, the leader invites people who sense a resonance with the gate's purpose to leave their seat and stand at the gate. Often people find themselves drawn to more than one gate.

The interactive dynamic of the presentation is invaluable. It gives participants the opportunity to respond to each gate's purpose, while being prayed for and praying for others. Seeing others at the gate, who identify the same gift is immediate affirmation. A token of remembrance may also be given to people who identify with a gate. It is a tangible reminder of a spiritual insight. Each gate's presentation concludes with prayer and a blessing that nudges people forward in spiritual growth. The sum total of the experience is strong encouragement for believers to press into all that God has entrusted to them.

SCRIPT

The worship space is arranged in a rectangle with the congregation seated on three sides. The Music Ministry occupies the fourth side. In the center of the rectangle is a large canvas map of the city of Jerusalem at the time of Nehemiah. The city's' ten gates are clearly marked on the map. A representation of the Ark of the Covenant is placed in the location of the Temple. The Ark is used as the Communion Table for the celebration of the Lord's Supper, which may or may not be included according to your tradition.

The presentation team consists of the Leader (often a pastor*), two assistants, six script readers* (best recruited from Youth Group members)*, the Music Ministry, sound and power-point engineers.*

The Leader's part is scripted with allowance for impromptu comments that facilitate and enhance the flow of the presentation.

Each gate is identified with a sign containing the name of the gate and highlights of its significance. It adds to the fun to have a visual representation of each gate, i.e., Dung Gate – a garbage can, Sheep gate – a toy sheep, Old Gate – a Church history book, Valley gate – a box of Kleenex, etc. Pertinent power-point material is projected on overhead screens.

The presentation may be divided into parts offered on successive Sunday mornings in place of the sermon, or as a whole over approximately 2 hours. This script is written for a three-part option.

After the Leader prays for the people who have identified a gate as their place of gifting and ministry, he gives them a token of remembrance, like a prayer card, Pocket Cross, book mark, etc.

Rehearsals are held as needed to prepare for the presentation.

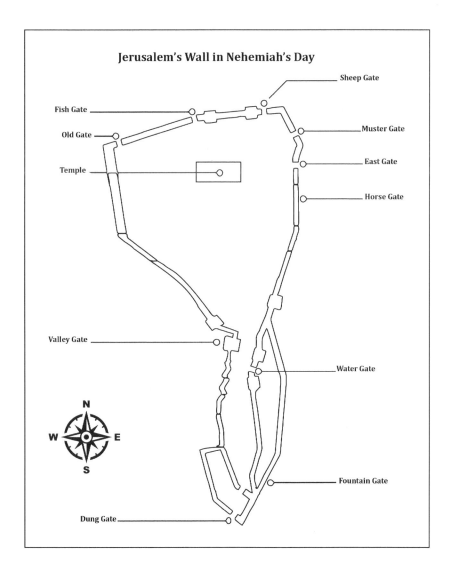

FIRST SUNDAY
INTRODUCTION — THE BOOK OF NEHEMIAH

READER 1 – Welcome! Mapped out on the floor is the holy city of Jerusalem as it was at the time of Nehemiah and Ezra in the 5th century BC. Today and for the next two Sundays, instead of a sermon, we will explore the ten gates of the walled city of Jerusalem. On our adventure we will encounter God's purpose for the gates, Jesus' ministry reflected in the gates, and our ministry for the kingdom of God today. Learn which of the Holy City's gates resonates with your heart and best expresses the gifts God has entrusted to you. Determine which gate aligns with your sense of witness, ministry, and mission for God's kingdom.

(Power Point: Introducing the Ten Gates)

READER 3 – **The ten gates of Nehemiah's Jerusalem are a call to evangelism which Jesus summarized in his Great Commission:** *"Go and make disciples of all nations, baptizing them in the name of the Father and of the Son and of the Holy Spirit, and teaching them to obey everything I have commanded you. I am with you always, to the very end of the age."* [139]

READER 2 – Before we begin, I invite you to greet your fellow explorers by passing the Peace. A friendly "hey", handshake, or embrace is appropriate, along with the words…

---

139   Matthew 28:19-20

(Power Point: order of worship)

READER 2 – The Peace of Christ be with you.

PEOPLE – And also with you.

(Pause while the Peace is passed.)

READER 1 – We will focus on Chapter 3 of the Book of Nehemiah. It's helpful to think of this as a first person memoir written by a Jewish man who was the "cupbearer to the king", a high position in the Persian Court.

READER 2 – In 586 BC, the Persian Empire defeated Israel, and took a multitude captive into exile. In the 20th year of the reign of Artaxerxes, about 70 years after the Jewish people had been released from captivity, Nehemiah learned that Jerusalem was still in shambles. He also found out that there was a famine in the land. The news deeply troubled him.

READER 3 – God placed a burden for Israel on Nehemiah's heart. He mourned, fasted, and cried out to God in prayer, confessing Israel's sins, reminding God of His promise to restore His people to the Promised Land.

READER 5 – Emboldened by God, Nehemiah asked King Artaxerxes' permission to return to Jerusalem and rebuild the city's walls. The King not only agreed to the request; he gave significant aid to the mission.

READER 4 – Jerusalem was still occupied by a remnant population of Israelites who had not been taken captive.

Carrying letters of authorization from the king, Nehemiah traveled to Jerusalem in 445 BC to inspect the walls, make a plan for their restoration, and organize the people to begin the work.

READER 5 – With the help of the high priest, Eliashib, and the priest, Ezra, Nehemiah organized the Jewish citizens to begin reconstruction.

READER 6 – At the same time, the neighboring enemies of Jerusalem, the Samaritans, the Ammonites, and the Arabs, plotted to attack and take the city. Nehemiah urged the people to work with weapons in one hand and tools in the other.

READER 3 – Nehemiah acted as civil governor despite opposition from enemies, and even resistance from Jewish officials in Jerusalem. People don't like change. Nehemiah oversaw the rebuilding of the walls. He also brought about reform to the city in conformity with the Law of Moses. He eventually appointed new officials, set guards on the walls and at the gates, made plans to register the Jews, and with the help of the Levites, found the lost Census of those who had returned earlier.

READER 2 – Ezra, a priest and ally in the reconstruction, had been in Jerusalem teaching the Scriptures for fourteen years. After the walls were rebuilt, Nehemiah assembled the people in penance and asked Ezra to read from the Law of Moses. In response, the people confessed past sins, agreed to separate themselves from the surrounding people, and keep the Law of Moses. In addition, the Levites instituted the Feast of Booths in accordance with the Law.

READER 4 – Eventually, Jerusalem was repopulated by Israelites from the towns and villages of Judah and Benjamin. This was no small project. After twelve years of hard labor, Nehemiah returned to the Persian capital of Susa. Years later he learned that the Israelites in Jerusalem had become unfaithful to God. Nehemiah returned to the city to enforce the Law.

LEADER – In rebuilding the walls, Nehemiah restored the ten gates that led into and out of Jerusalem. The gates listed in chapter 3 serve as a metaphor, revealing ten ways people come to Jesus Christ and go out to fulfill his Great Commission.

READER 1 – The Book of Ruth illustrates how a city's gates functioned for protection, commerce, and a place of government.

READER 3 – Boaz desired to marry Ruth, but that right belonged to her nearest kinsman-redeemer. Boaz waited for that man to come to the city gate. When the kinsman-redeemer relinquished his right to marry Ruth, Boaz gathered the town's ten elders at the main gate and announced that he would buy Naomi's land and marry Ruth.[140]

READER 4 – The city elders at the gate not only witnessed the legal transfer of property, but also prayed a blessing over Ruth and Boaz's marriage. The city gate was the place of protection and blessing.

140   Ruth 4:1-11

READER 2 – Cities are no longer protected by literal stone walls and iron gates. Today's walls and gates are the Mayor, City Council, Police Department, Fire Department, Courthouse, Board of Education, Ministerial Association, and community organizations.

LEADER – A city's walls and gates consist of people who are organized to oversee and protect aspects of a community's life for the common good.

Likewise, every congregation has gates, often reflecting the strengths of the congregation's leadership. God calls different people to different gates for different aspects of ministry. This is part of God's design, which begins with God calling a person. When the call is accepted, God purposefully forms a disciple to stand at a gate. Paul understood this when he wrote:... *when God, who set me apart from birth and called me by his grace, was pleased to reveal his Son in me so that I might preach him among the Gentiles....*[141]

READER 2 — The Gates represent different aspects of the ministry and mission of Jesus and of His Body, the Church. How well do we resemble Him? Lets take a quick look at the ten gates of Jerusalem in the days of Nehemiah and the ways they reveal Jesus.

---

141   Galatians 1:15-17

THE PURPOSE OF THE GATES
(Power Point)

The Gates are places of Decision

- All ten Gates have an evangelical and specific ministry purpose.
- The Gates reveal the heart and passion of Jesus – that all would come within his loving and saving embrace.

READER 4 – In the Bible **"ten"** is the number of divine order, as in the Ten Commandments. Jesus lived in perfect divine order, fulfilling the requirements of the law and the prophets.

READER 2 — The gates are **entry** and **exit points** to the City of God. The City walls are for **security**. Unwalled cities were vulnerable. The prophet Isaiah wrote that the people are to call the *"walls Salvation and our gates Praise."* [142]

The gates facilitate **traffic** into and out of the city. While the Temple was the heart of Jerusalem, the gates proclaimed God's **glory** and sovereignty, attracting pilgrims and visitors.

READER 3 — The gates are also places of **decision** and **commitment**. Elders of the city sat at the gates making legal and political decisions concerning the city, its traffic and commerce. [143] People came through the gates into Je-

---

142   Isaiah 60:18
143   Ruth 4:11-12

rusalem and the presence of God. In turn, they went out from the presence of God through the city gates into the world. Entering and leaving is a process of making significant decisions and commitments regarding our life's purpose; our stewardship of the gifts entrusted to us; and our willingness to be obedient to His will.

READER 6 – Please remember, becoming Jesus' disciple is a life-long **process** of learning and serving. It is filled with events, decisions and commitments that mature our character. Our character enables people to hear Jesus in what we say and see Jesus in what we do.

READER 1 — All ten gates are established with the **evangelical purpose** of reaching people who have become disconnected or are completely outside the Kingdom of God. Each gate was established with a specific ministry purpose. The gates reveal the heart and passion of Jesus that all would come within His loving, saving embrace, and move from the darkness of the world into the eternal light of the City of God.

READER 3 — Today, listen to the purpose for each gate; determine whether it is consistent with your sense of mission and the gifts you believe God has given you. If so, go to that gate and stand with other believers with similar gifting. As you explore your place in the city of God, you may respond to more than one City Gate. This is not unusual. Exploring the gates gives us the opportunity to look into our own heart, as well as the heart of God.

(Power Point: Ministries of the Ten Gates)

1 – Sheep Gate: Healing
2 – Fish Gate: Fishers of Men through Friendship
3 – Old Gate: History & Traditions
4 – Valley Gate: Comfort & Mercy
5 – Dung Gate: Confession of Sins
6 – Fountain Gate: Renewal of the Holy Spirit
7 – Water Gate: Biblical Preaching and Teaching
8 – Horse Gate: Spiritual Warfare
9 – East Gate: The Presence of God
10 – Muster Gate: Holiness of Life

READER 1 — Which gates are the strengths of your church's leadership? Which gates express the ministries of your church? Through which gates do you most often come into God's presence and go out into the world?

READER 2 — The Sheep Gate, Valley Gate, Muster Gate and East Gate are common to all churches, but some branches of the church place special emphasis on certain gates.

(Power Point: The Gates in the Church today.)

Evangelical Churches:
   Water Gate: Word of God
   Fish Gate: Fishers of Men through Friendship
   Evangelism
Pentecostal Churches:
   Fountain Gate: Gifts and Fruit of the Holy Spirit
   Horse Gate: Spiritual Warfare

Sacramental Churches:
Old Gate: History and Traditions
Dung Gate: Confession, Repentance and
Forgiveness

No branch of the church, let alone any congregation, has it all. The Body of Christ is the whole Church, not bits and pieces. We need each other and are called by Jesus to be in relational unity.

READER 3 – Before Jesus went to the Cross; He prayed that we would all be one. Listen to the closing words of His prayer for His disciples — then and now: *"My prayer is not for them alone. I pray also for those who will believe in me through their message, that all of them may be one, Father, just as you are in me and I am in you. May they also be in us so that the world may believe that you have sent me. I have given them the glory that you gave me, that they may be one as we are one: I in them and you in me—so that they may be brought to complete unity. Then the world will know that you sent me and have loved them even as you have loved me."*[144]

READER 4 – I'm ready to explore a gate.

READER 1 – Me too!

READER 4 – Where should we start?

LEADER – We begin with the **SHEEP GATE** and go around Jerusalem's walls counter-clock-wise.

---

144   John 17:20-23

1. SHEEP GATE: SALVATION & HEALING

(Power Point)

> **SHEEP GATE**
> **Salvation & Healing**
>
> - Jesus heals our relationship with God
> - Salvation is the first and greatest of all healings
>   - **1 Pet 2:24** *He himself bore our sins in his body on the tree, so that we might die to sins and live for righteousness; by his wounds you have been healed.*

READER 6 – In **Nehemiah 3:1-2** we read that: *Eliashib the high priest* (whose name means God restores) *and his fellow priests went to work and rebuilt the Sheep Gate.*

It is a gate in the eastern wall and was the first gate to be rebuilt. It is also the last gate mentioned in the list of gates, making the Sheep Gate both the beginning and the ending point of the wall. This is most likely because the Sheep Gate was the way sacrificial offerings were brought into the Temple.

READER 4 – The metaphor of this first and last gate tells us who we are and to whom we belong. Jesus taught, *"I am the good shepherd; I know my sheep and my sheep know me... and I lay down my life for the sheep."*[145] We are the sheep. Jesus is our Good Shepherd.

---

145   John 10:14-15

READER 2 – At the same time, in the Bible sheep and lambs are symbols of Christ: *"The next day John saw Jesus coming toward him and said, 'Look, the Lamb of God, who takes away the sin of the world!'"* [146] Like the Sheep Gate, which was the starting and ending point of Jerusalem's wall, Jesus Christ is the starting (alpha) and ending point (omega) of everything.

READER 5 – In Jesus' day the Pool of Bethesda was right outside the Sheep Gate. In John's Gospel we read:... *Jesus went up to Jerusalem for a feast of the Jews. Now there is in Jerusalem near the Sheep Gate a pool... called Bethesda (meaning house of grace).... Here a great number of disabled people used to lie — the blind, the lame, the paralyzed. One who was there had been an invalid for thirty-eight years. When Jesus saw him lying there and learned that he had been in this condition for a long time, he asked him, "Do you want to get well?"*

"Sir," the invalid replied, "I have no one to help me into the pool when the water is stirred. While I am trying to get in, someone else goes down ahead of me."

Then Jesus said to him, "Get up! Pick up your mat and walk." At once the man was cured; he picked up his mat and walked."[147]

READER 4 – Jesus, in His grace, heals our relationship with God. He also heals the disease and brokenness in our body, soul and spirit. He is our Good Shepherd. We are the

---

146   John 1:29
147   John 5:1-9 addition mine

sheep of His pasture. He knows us, loves us, and laid down His life for us.[148]

READER 3 — His death on the Cross opens gates in the walls of salvation for all who put their faith in Him. In Peter's first epistle, he writes: *His* (Jesus') *wounds became your healing.*[149]

To personally know Jesus as Savior and Lord is the first and greatest healing. The Good News is that our Lord Jesus loves, accepts and forgives us. At the Cross He paid our sin debt, won for us victory, and secured for us eternal life.

LEADER – Have you passed through the Sheep Gate? Have you made a personal decision to accept Jesus Christ as your Savior and Lord? Do you remember when that happened, and where you were? Was there a person who was instrumental in your coming to that starting point in your Christian journey? Perhaps you were raised in a Christian home, baptized as an infant, and can't remember when Jesus wasn't part of your life.

If you would like to reaffirm your commitment to Jesus Christ, or if you haven't yet made that decision and would like to do that right now, repeat this prayer after me:

(Power Point: Order of Worship)

Dear Jesus... *(repeat)...* I am a sinner... *(repeat)...* I repent of my sins... *(repeat)...* Please forgive me and save me by your shed blood... *(repeat)...* come into my heart...

---

148   John 10:11 & 14
149   1 Peter 2:24 addition mine

(repeat)... I want to receive you as my own personal Lord and Savior... *(repeat)...* Amen... *(repeat)*.

(Pause to see if all is well.)

LEADER – If you just prayed that prayer for the first time in your life, please tell someone here about it before you leave. It's an important way of taking a first step in faith with Jesus, and the person you tell will be blessed.

The Holy Spirit's gifts of faith, healing, and miracles are frequently manifest at the Sheep Gate. Answered prayer, signs, and wonders are the fruit of ministry in this place. If you are a health care professional, therapist, counselor, social worker, pastor or chaplain this gate may resonate with your heart and God's call upon your life. If you visit and pray with people who have shared their needs - the troubled, shut-ins, prisoners, the sick and suffering, this may be your gate assignment.

It is here that believers coming and going witness to their Christian faith and minister the healing touch of Jesus with prayer, laying-on of hands, and anointing with Holy Oil.

Ask the Lord if the Sheep Gate is you assignment.

INVITATION – RESPONSE – MUSIC – PRAYER

The Leader invites everyone who believes the Sheep Gate to be his or her assignment to come and stand at the gate. Time is given for people to respond, while the Music Ministry softly offers an appropriate hymn or praise song.

The Leader invites the Readers to place their hands on the shoulders of their brothers and sisters. The congregation is asked to extend their hands toward the people at the Sheep Gate.

The Leader offers a prayer of thanksgiving and blessing that their ministry would be repeatedly confirmed, that they grow in character and competence, and that they see abundant evidence of answered prayer, bringing all the glory to God.

The Leader gives each person who responded to the Sheep Gate invitation a prayer card with a picture of Jesus on one side and John 10:14-15 on the other.

2. FISH GATE: FISHERS OF MEN
THROUGH FRIENDSHIP

(Power Point)

FISH GATE
Friendship

- **Matt 4:18-20** *"Come, follow me," Jesus said, "and I will make you fishers of men." At once they left their nets and followed him.*
- Friendship with God: Father, Son and Holy Spirit
- Evangelism: Make a friend. Be a friend. Bring a friend to Jesus.
- The Fish Gate is also the "narrow gate" in **Matt 7:13-14**

READER 3 — In **Nehemiah 3:3**, we read: *The Fish Gate was rebuilt by the sons of Hassenaah. They laid its beams and put its doors and bolts and bars in place.* The Fish Gate was in the north wall, close to a fish market where fishermen from the Sea of Galilee and the Jordon River would come to sell their catch.

READER 4 – At the Sheep Gate we were introduced to Jesus Christ. There we discovered who we are and to whom we belong. At the Fish Gate we talk to others about Jesus: sometimes to family, friends and neighbors; sometimes to strangers; sometimes to many; sometimes one on one.

Before ascending into heaven, Jesus told His followers: *"Therefore go and make disciples of all nations, baptizing them in the name of the Father and of the Son and of the Holy Spirit, and teaching them to obey everything I have commanded you. And surely I am with you always, to the very end of the age."* [150]

READER 3 – The Gospel of Matthew tells us that: *As Jesus was walking beside the Sea of Galilee, he saw two brothers, Simon called Peter and his brother Andrew. They were casting a net into the lake, for they were fishermen. "Come, follow me," Jesus said, "and I will make you fishers of men." At once they left their nets and followed him.* [151]

READER 1 — Simon Peter and Andrew left their nets and boat in response to Jesus' invitation for them to become *"fishers of men."* It is significant that *"at once they left their nets and followed him."*

---

150   Matthew 28:19-20
151   Matthew 4:18-20

READER 2 – As fishers of men, it is essential to understand a person's culture and needs while honoring their freedom to make a decision for Christ. We also must know what we offer: our friendship and the opportunity for an eternal friendship with Jesus Christ. Genuine friendship is the key to becoming fishers of men and women.

READER 1 – Here's the truly astounding thing; Jesus chooses you and counts you as His friend. It is a friendship grounded in love and built upon the foundation of obedience to Him, just as Jesus has kept His Father's commandments and remains in His love. It is a friendship that gives us the privilege of using Jesus' name when asking anything of God the Father in prayer. It is a friendship that will bear lasting fruit in your life, in the lives of others, and ultimately render glory to God.[152]

READER 1 – Wait a minute! I thought God loves us unconditionally, but you just said that Jesus' love for us is based on obedience. Isn't that a condition?

READER 4 – Yes and no, Jesus said: *This is my command: Love each other.*[153] Love is the energy that makes the Fish Gate work. God loves us even if we don't choose to be obedient to His will, but our disobedience hinders God's ability to work in and through us.

READER 1 — Everyone is welcome to enter the City of God. Everyone within the City is encouraged to minister at the Fish Gate, making new friends and introducing them to our best friend, Jesus Christ. The city where we

152   John 15:9-16
153   John 15:17

live is our primary mission field. But some believers will go out from the Fish Gate to make new friends and share the Good News in far away places.

LEADER — There is also a paradox in the Fish Gate. It is the *"narrow gate"* that Jesus speaks of in Matthew's Gospel: *"Enter through the narrow gate. For wide is the gate and broad is the road that leads to destruction, and many enter through it. But small is the gate and narrow the road that leads to life, and only a few find it."* [154]

Jesus personalizes the gate image when He tells His disciples, *"I am the way and the truth and the life. No one comes to the Father except through me."* [155]

Do you have a friendship with Jesus? Are you willing to introduce your friend Jesus to someone who doesn't know Him, but is searching for truth, meaning and purpose in their life? If your answer is yes, the Fish Gate is certainly part of your assignment. Come and stand at the Fish Gate. Bible study, home fellowship, and small group hosts, leaders, and members are found at the Fish Gate. They welcome people into the presence of God, facilitate friendships, and build unity within the church. Come, this is your gate.

INVITATION – RESPONSE – MUSIC – PRAYER

The Leader invites people who stood at the Sheep Gate to come and place their hand on the shoulder of their brothers and sisters at the Fish Gate. The congregation

---

154   Matthew 7:13-14
155   John 14:6

is asked to extend their hands toward the people at the Fish Gate.

The Leader offers a prayer of thanksgiving and blessing that their calling would be repeatedly confirmed, that they would grow in character and competence in the ministry of friendship and evangelism, that their witness would be fruitful and bring God glory.

The Leader gives each person at the Fish Gate a prayer card with a picture of Jesus on one side and "The Sinner's Prayer" printed on the other side.

3. OLD GATE: HISTORY & TRADITIONS

(Power Point)

OLD GATE
Sacraments, Traditions & Church History

- *Jesus is the Lamb that was slain from the creation of the world.* **Rev 13:8**
- *He is the same yesterday and today and forever.* **Heb 13:8**

READER 1 — In **Nehemiah 3:6**, we read: *The Jeshanah Gate (or Old Gate) was repaired by Joiada... and Meshullam... They laid its beams and put its doors and bolts and bars in place.*

READER 4 — We live in a culture predisposed to youth that subtly devalues age. We are a people who exist in a transitory world where we live in and for the moment with little connection to our heritage. We are suspicious of the past, judging it to be dead, or at least stale, musty, unattractive and possibly unhealthy.

READER 2 – The "old" can also embody that which is solid, stable, proven and of high value. In the book of Deuteronomy, Israel was urged to: *Remember the days of old; consider the generations long past.*[156] God's people often forgot their history and the many times God's hand was mighty to save them from perilous circumstances. The prophet Jeremiah admonished the often stubborn and forgetful Israelites, *"Stand at the crossroads and look; ask where the good way is, and walk in it, and you will find rest for your souls.*[157] When God's people looked back and remembered God's intervention at the Passover and the parting the Red Sea, they were strongly encouraged.

READER 3 — The Old Gate is beautiful and ornate. It proclaims the amazing grace of salvation's history flowing through the Old and New Testaments and the tumultuous, courageous story of the Church. The Old Gate reveals Jesus Christ and embodies the liturgies and sacraments of the Judaic/Christian traditions. It embraces the theology, doctrine, art, architecture, literature, music, dance and drama that reveal Jesus Christ and comprise our Christian heritage.

---

156 Deuteronomy 32:7
157 Jeremiah 6:16

READER 1 — The prophet Daniel tells us that God is the Ancient of Days.[158] His Son Jesus is:... *the Lamb that was slain from the creation of the world.*[159] Scripture also tells us that Jesus... *is the same yesterday and today and forever.*[160] God is constant and unchanging in our lives, which are transitory and sometimes filled with discouragement.

READER 4 – We are not alone. God is with us. His Holy Spirit lives in us. And we have brothers and sisters in the Body of Christ to hold up our arms, to pray for and with us. They give us encouragement. Remember, the author of the book of Hebrews writes:... *encourage one another daily, as long as it is called Today, so that none of you may be hardened by sin's deceitfulness. We have come to share in Christ if we hold firmly till the end the confidence we had at first.*[161] REMEMBER!

LEADER – If you are an encourager in the faith, a person who listens to others attentively and compassionately, the Old Gate is where you belong. It is also the gate for people who see the reality of God in looking through a telescope, in the results of a lab experiment, in the mystery of a computer chip, in the dynamics of a classroom, or in the beauty of nature. Your declaration of God's unchanging truth brings encouragement to others.

The Old Gate is the place of ministry for people of academic, artistic, and scientific vocations –teachers, students, historians, engineers, scientists – people who value

---

158   Daniel 7:9, 13, 22
159   Revelation 13:8
160   Hebrews 13:8
161   Hebrews 3:13 -14

and pursue connections, continuity, history and enduring beauty.

Do you enter and exit the City of God through the Old Gate? Is the Old Gate your assignment? Come and stand at the Old Gate.

INVITATION – RESPONSE – MUSIC – PRAYER

The Leader invites those who stood at the Fish Gate to stand with the people gathered at the Old Gate and place their hand on the shoulder of their brothers and sisters. The congregation is asked to extend their hands toward the people gathered at the Old Gate.

The Leader offers a prayer of thanksgiving and blessing upon them that their calling would be repeatedly confirmed, that they would grow in character, competence, and creativity in their field, that the Holy Spirit would be their inspiration, and that everything they are and do would bring God glory.

The Leader gives each person at the Old Gate a bookmark with picture of Michelangelo's hand of God touching the hand of Adam. On the other side, the Venite: Psalm 95:1-7; 96: 9,13.

LEADER – Next Sunday we will explore four more gates of Nehemiah's Jerusalem: The Valley Gate, The Dung Gate, The Fountain Gate and Water Gate. The following and final Sunday of this series, we will explore The Horse Gate, The East or Golden Gate, and The Muster Gate.

I invite those who came to one or more of this morning's three gates to raise their hand. If you are near a person with their hand up, place your hand on their shoulder as we pray together:

(Power Point: Order of Worship)

LEADER & PEOPLE —

Heavenly Father,

We humble ourselves before You.

Thank You for calling and blessing us.

We purpose to be good stewards of the ministry gifts You give.

We will serve at the gate to which You have assigned us.

Father, please expand our spheres of influence.

Keep Your Hand upon us at all times.

Protect us from evil and harm and from causing others pain.

Bless us to be a blessing to others

As Your witnesses, ministers, and missionaries

To advance Your kingdom and bring You glory.

We ask this in Jesus' Name. Amen.

SECOND SUNDAY
REVIEW

READER 1 – Good Morning! We are going to return to the Book of Nehemiah, chapter 3, which is the account of Nehemiah's journey to Jerusalem where he lead the Israelites in rebuilding the walls and gates of the city.

Before we begin, I invite you to greet your fellow travelers by passing the Peace. A friendly handshake, or embrace is appropriate, along with the words…

(Power Point: Order of Worship)

READER 1 – The Peace of Christ be with you.

PEOPLE – And also with you.

(Pause while the Peace is passed.)

(Power Point)

REVIEW

- **The GATES are places of Traffic**
  - Evangelical Purpose
    - o Invitations,
    - o Decisions
- **Purpose of the GATES**
  - Sheep Gate: Healing
  - Fish Gate: Fishers of Men/Friendship
  - Old Gate: History & Traditions of the Church
- **The GATES grow Leaders**
  - Influential
  - Life-long Learners
  - Trustworthy

READER 2 — The ten gates of Jerusalem reveal the heart and passion of Jesus and His ministry. The gates also help us discern God's purpose for our life, identify His gifts for ministry, and outline a pattern for evangelism and mission. Each gate presents us with an **invitation**, and challenges us to make a **decision**.

READER 3 — The gates enable **traffic** to enter and exit the city. People come and go in response to the gate's location and purpose, as well as their need. As believers identify God's call on their life and mature in the gifts He has given them, they minister at the corresponding gate. Competence in their gifts allows people to pass through the gates to minister in a mission field outside the City of God.

READER 4 — Each gate was established with a purpose. Last Sunday we explored the…

(Read and Power Point: First Three Gates)

- **SHEEP GATE: HEALING** – health care professionals, therapists, counselors, pastors and chaplains, Bible study and small group leaders, believers who pray for and with others.

- **FISH GATE: FISHERS OF MEN** – evangelism, make a friend, be a friend, bring your friend to Jesus.

- **OLD GATE: HISTORY & TRADITIONS** – proclaiming ancient truths of God's creation and humanity's history and traditions. This includes the academic, scientific and artistic vocations that value and pursue connections, continuity, enduring truth and beauty.

LEADER — If you were here last Sunday and came forward to stand at a gate, I invite you to return and stand at that gate right now. If you stood at more than one gate, please go to the gate that is the most significant for you.

The Leader invites people to the gates as a refresher and to model the appropriate response for the coming invitations. The Leader invites those in the congregation to extend their hands toward those at the gates and prays an extemporaneous blessing on the people standing at the gates before they return to their seats.

READER 6 – Nehemiah is a leader of God's people. He teaches us three lessons about leadership.

The true measure of leadership is **influence**, not a title. We see that Nehemiah had considerable influence with the Babylonian King, Artaxerxes. In Jerusalem he developed influence with the High Priest Eliashib and the priest Ezra, but his greatest influence was over the Jewish people and even their enemies.

READER 5 — Leaders are **life long learners**. Leadership is a complex process of developing skills and nurturing character that requires time and practice. During the twelve years it took Nehemiah to lead the restoration of Jerusalem's walls and gates, he daily grew in leadership skills, which is evidenced by the fact that before returning to Babylonia he was able to initiate reforms and had the people rededicate themselves to God and the Law of Moses.

READER 2 — **Trust** is the foundation of leadership. When a leader breaks trust, he or she forfeits their ability to lead. The Jewish people came to trust Nehemiah's leadership to the point of putting their lives in peril at Nehemiah's command. Because their enemies were all around them, they rebuilt the walls with tools in one hand and weapons in the other.

READER 1 – Lets explore four more gates: The Valley Gate, The Dung Gate, The Fountain Gate and Water Gate.

4. VALLEY GATE: COMFORT & MERCY TO THOSE IN SORROW, CRISIS, OR NEED

(Power Point)

VALLEY GATE
Comfort & Mercy to those in Sorrow, Crisis or Need

- The Valley Gate is the door of hope in the midst of trouble and affliction that leads to the presence of God.
- **Psalm 23:4** *"Even though I walk through the valley of the shadow of death, I will fear no evil, for you are with me; your rod and staff, they comfort me."*

READER 4 – Nehemiah 3:13 tells us that: *The Valley Gate was repaired by Hanun and the residents of Zanoah. They rebuilt it and put its doors and bolts and bars in place. They also repaired five hundred yards of the wall as far as the Dung Gate.*

The wall from the Old Gate to the Valley Gate is a considerable distance. It is 450 meters from the Valley Gate to the Dung Gate. This means that the Valley Gate stands alone in a vast expanse of wall.

READER 2 – Valleys can be dark, lonely places of sorrow and humbling experiences. The Bible uses the word "valley" metaphorically to describe times of discouragement and trials, reminding us of the words in the **23rd Psalm**: *"Even though I walk through the darkest valley, I will fear no evil, for you are with me; your rod and your staff, they comfort me."*[162] The Valley Gate is the gateway of hope in the midst of trouble and affliction.

READER 3 – Being a Christian isn't easy! We are told: *"In this world you will have trouble."* [163]

READER 1 – Jesus read these words from the scroll of Isaiah: *"The Spirit of the Lord is on me, because he has anointed me to preach good news to the poor. He has sent me to proclaim freedom for the prisoners and recovery of sight for the blind, to release the oppressed, to proclaim the year of the Lord's favor."* Then he rolled up the scroll, gave it back to the attendant and sat down. The eyes of everyone in the

---

162   Psalm 23:4
163   John 16:33a

synagogue were fastened on him, and he began by saying to them, "Today this scripture is fulfilled in your hearing." [164]

READER 5 – Jesus in His love established a gate of mercy and hope, so that we will not be overcome by doubt and discouragement. He says to us: *"But take heart! I have overcome the world."* [165]

READER 6 – The sections of wall are long and dark before and after the Valley Gate. New Christians and life-long believers alike can succumb to a valley's darkness and despair. These are times when it's essential to remain close to the Lord and cling to the promise given by Paul, who endured much for the sake of Christ: *"No temptation has overtaken you except what is common to mankind. And God is faithful; he will not let you be tempted beyond what you can bear. But when you are tempted, he will also provide a way out so that you can endure it."* [166]

LEADER — The Valley Gate is ministry to people in desperate need of basic things: food, clothing, shelter, and non-judgmental, trustworthy friendship – a helping heart and hand.

Are you called to the Valley Gate to be with those who are traveling through the valleys of life in need of God's tenderness and mercy? Is your ministry to the unemployed, the elderly, the homeless, the grieving, the poor, refugees, people with disabilities, or the mentally ill?

---

164   Luke 4:18-21
165   Luke 3:5
166   1 Corinthians 10:13

Local, state and national government officials and those in the legal profession are called to stand at the Valley Gate, providing order, justice, and mercy. Is your ministry to the victims of abuse, prisoners, or those wrestling with addiction? Are you willing to be present for the brother or sister in Christ, family member, friend, neighbor or stranger who is struggling? Did you yourself enter the City of God through the Valley Gate? Are you called to stand at the "Door of Hope" in life's Valleys to provide to others the comfort you received from God?[167]

INVITATION - RESPONSE - MUSIC - PRAYER

The Leader invites the people who stood at the Old Gate last week to join those gathered at the Valley Gate and place their hand on a brother or sister's shoulder. The congregation is asked to extend their hands toward the people at the Valley Gate.

The Leader offers a prayer of thanksgiving and blessing upon them: asking that their calling would be repeatedly confirmed; that their thoughts, words and actions would reveal Jesus's tender mercies and truth; that the Holy Spirit would be their guide; and that in every encounter they would bring comfort and provision to those God puts on their path — all to God's glory.

The Leader gives each person at the Valley Gate a Pocket Cross.

---

167   2 Corinthians 1:4

5. DUNG GATE: REPENTANCE, CONFESSION, AND FORGIVING OTHERS

(Power Point)

DUNG or REFUSE GATE

Conviction, Confession of Sin with Repentance & Forgiving Others

- The place where we "dump our junk"
- **Isa 1:18-19** the Lord assures us, *"Though your sins are like scarlet, they shall be as white as snow…. If you are willing and obedient, you will eat the best from the land…."*
- **1 John 1:8-9** & **James 5:16**

READER 4 — In **Nehemiah 3:14** we read: *"The Dung Gate was repaired by Malkijah… He rebuilt it and put its doors and bolts and bars in place."* To be blunt, this gate led to the place where Jerusalem dumped and burned garbage.

READERS 1 – Yuck!

READER 3 – That's gross.

READER 2 – Yes, but when we make the decision to surrender our life to Jesus Christ, we must begin to clear the clutter and take our garbage to the dump. Often the trials and tribulations we have identified at the Valley Gate highlight the junk that has accumulated and should be taken to the dump and burned.

READER 4 – Sin is garbage. **1 John 1:8-9**, admonishes us: *If we claim to be without sin, we deceive ourselves and the truth is not in us. If we confess our sins, he is faithful and just and will forgive us our sins and purify us from all unrighteousness.*

READER 1 — **James 5:16**, further instructs us:… *confess your sins to each other and pray for each other so that you may be healed. The prayer of a righteous man is powerful and effective.*

READER 3 – In the Lord's Prayer, Jesus taught that we are to ask our heavenly Father's forgiveness for our sins – done and left undone – and also to forgive those who have sinned against us. To emphasize the importance of asking God's forgiveness and forgiving others, Jesus said, *"For if you forgive other people when they sin against you, your heavenly Father will also forgive you."* [168]

READER 5 – Paul uses the analogy of old leaven to describe sin that is to be replaced with the unleavened bread of righteousness in Christ. Throughout Paul's letters, he refers to the old self as our sinful nature, and the new self as our new nature in Christ.

READER 6 – Sin is the garbage that needs to be sorted out and disposed of. Things like our old practices[169] of malice, wickedness,[170] deceitful desires,[171] and the obvious acts of the sinful nature as listed in Galatians: *"sexual immorality,*

---

168 Matthew 6:12+14
169 Colossians 3:9
170 1 Corinthians 5:8
171 Ephesians 4:22

impurity and debauchery; idolatry and witchcraft; hatred, discord, jealousy, fits of rage, selfish ambition, dissentions, factions and envy; drunkenness, orgies, and the like." [172]

READER 2 – When Jesus confronted the Samaritan woman at the well with her sin, the Holy Spirit brought conviction and repentance to her heart. Jesus forgave her sins. As a result she invited her whole village to meet Jesus, her new friend and master.[173] Because of her witness many people came to faith and salvation in Jesus Christ.

READER 4 – Paul underlines the importance of the Dung Gate when he writes: *All this is from God, who reconciled us to himself through Christ and gave us the ministry of reconciliation: that God was reconciling the world to himself in Christ, not counting men's sins against them. And he has committed to us the message of reconciliation. We are therefore Christ's ambassadors, as though God were making his appeal through us. We implore you on Christ's behalf: Be reconciled to God. God made him who had no sin to be sin for us, so that in him we might become the righteousness of God.*[174]

READER 2 – Twice in the Gospel of Matthew, Jesus promises His disciples: *I will give you the keys of the kingdom of heaven; whatever you bind on earth will be bound in heaven, and whatever you loose on earth will be loosed in heaven.*[175] Forgiveness and forgiving others looses us from sin allowing us to stand in Victory. Bible study, prayer, fellowship,

172   Galatians 5:17-21
173   Luke 7:36-50
174   2 Corinthians 5:17-21
175   Matthew 16:19 & 18:18

and worship are some of the things that bind us to God and His Kingdom.

LEADER — Do you long to lift the downcast heads of sinners and share Jesus' forgiveness that brings freedom from sin's burden? Are you willing to listen patiently, non-judgmentally to a person's repentant confession and offer them God's forgiveness? Will you encourage them to forgive people and situations that have wounded them? Do you yearn to see people set free from the bondages of sin that burden and destroy? Do you have a passion to help believers bind themselves to the things of God that build up rather than tear down? Then the Dung Gate is your gate.

INVITATION – RESPONSE – MUSIC – PRAYER

The Leader invites those who stood at the Valley Gate to come join the people gathered at the Dung Gate and place their hand on a shoulder. The congregation is asked to extend their hands toward the people at the Dung Gate.

The Leader offers a prayer of thanksgiving and blessing upon them: asking that their calling would be repeatedly confirmed; that their thoughts, words and actions would reveal Jesus's love, acceptance and forgiveness; that the Holy Spirit would be their guide; and that they would assist people in letting go of worldly things and in taking hold of the things of God — all to God's glory.

The Leader gives each person at the Dung Gate a prayer card with a picture of the crucifixion on one side and the Lord's Prayer, plus Matthew 6:14-15 & 18:18 printed on the other side.

READER 1 – The Dung Gate is where the population of Jerusalem dumped and burned their garbage, covering the ground with dust and ashes. In Genesis we are told that, *"the Lord God formed a man from the dust of the ground and breathed into his nostrils the breath of life, and the man became a living being."* [176]

READER 3 – As a result of Adam and Eve's sin of rebellion against God, they were expelled from Eden. The dire consequence of their sin was death.

READER 2 – During times of self-examination and penitence, especially at the beginning of Lent, we remember our mortality with the imposition of ashes and the words, *"Remember that you are dust, and to dust you shall return."* [177]

READER 4 – We also remember that it is only by the gracious gift of our Savior Jesus Christ's death on the Cross and resurrection from the grave that we are given everlasting life. *"Death has been swallowed up in victory,"* the apostle Paul declares. *"But thanks be to God! He gives us the victory through our Lord Jesus Christ."* [178]

LEADER – On Ash Wednesday, we use ashes from burned Palm Sunday branches to remind us of our mortality. Through Jesus' death and resurrection, we have victory over sin and death. Before we leave this gate, I invite you

---

176   Genesis 2:7
177   **1979 Book of Common Prayer**, page 265
178   1 Corinthians 15:54 & 57

to receive the imposition of ashes as an outward and visible sign of both your mortality and your Victory in Jesus Christ.

Two ministry assistants go to diagonal corners of the worship space with bowls of ashes. The Leader presents him or herself for the imposition of ashes to model the ministry response. People may present themselves for the imposition of ashes throughout the remainder of the presentation.

6. FOUNTAIN GATE: RENEWAL OF THE HOLY SPIRIT

(Power Point)

FOUNTAIN GATE
Renewal of the Holy Spirit

- This is entrance into Life in the Holy Spirit with the provision of the Gifts and Fruit
- **John 7: 37- 39** *"... Jesus stood and said in a loud voice, "Let anyone who is thirsty come to me and drink. Whoever believes in me, as Scripture has said, rivers of living water will flow from within them." By this he meant the Spirit, whom those who believed in him were later to receive.*

READER 4 – In **Nehemiah 3:15** we read: *The Fountain Gate was repaired by Shallun son of Kol-Hozeh, ruler of the district of Mizpah. He rebuilt it, roofing it over and putting its doors and bolts and bars in place. He also repaired the wall of the Pool of Siloam, by the King's Garden, as far as the steps going down from the City of David.*

READER 1 — In a parched land a water fountain is a luxury that proclaims abundance and refreshment. In a desert, water also represents power to the person who controls the rights to it.

READER 2 — In **Psalm 36**, David writes: *They feast on the abundance of your house; you give them drink from your river of delights. For with you is **the fountain of life**; in your light we see light.*[179]

READER 3 – The prophet Jeremiah describes God as a *fountain of living waters.*[180]

READER 5 — In speaking with the Samaritan woman at the well, Jesus combines these water images, *"fountain of life"* and *"living water,"* when He said to her, *"Everyone who drinks this water will be thirsty again, but whoever drinks the water I give him will never thirst. Indeed, the water I give him will become in him a spring of water welling up to eternal life."*

The woman said to him, "Sir, give me this water so that I won't get thirsty and have to keep coming here to draw water."[181]

---

179 Psalm 36:8-9 (the bold highlight is my addition)
180 Jeremiah 2:13
181 John 4:13-15

READER 3 — Later, on the last and greatest day of the Festival of Tabernacles, Jesus stood and said in a loud voice, *"If anyone is thirsty, let him come to me and drink. Whoever believes in me, as the Scripture has said, streams of living water will flow from within him." By this he meant the Spirit, whom those who believed in him were later to receive. Up to that time the Spirit had not been given, since Jesus had not yet been glorified.*[182]

READER 6 – The Bible contains many references to a fountain as a source of wisdom, fear of the Lord, righteousness, cleansing and renewal. The prophet Isaiah prophesied a time that Christians know as Pentecost: *"For I will pour water on the thirsty land, and streams on the dry ground; I will pour out my Spirit on your offspring, and my blessing on your descendants."*[183]

READER 5 – The Fountain Gate is the entrance into life in the Holy Spirit that John the Baptist prophesied when he said, *"I baptize you with water for repentance. But after me will come one who is more powerful than I, whose sandals I am not fit to carry. He will baptize you with the Holy Spirit and with fire."*[184]

READER 1 — Just before Pentecost, as Jesus was ascending into Heaven, He promised His disciples: ". . . *you will receive power when the Holy Spirit comes on you; and you will be my witnesses in Jerusalem, and in all Judea and Samaria, and to the ends of the earth."*[185]

---

182 John 7:37-39
183 Isaiah 44:3
184 Matthew 3:11-12
185 Acts 1:8

READER 4 — In **1 Corinthians**, Paul asks, *"Do you not know that your body is a temple of the Holy Spirit, who is in you, whom you have received from God?"* [186]

READER 6 — The Fountain Gate is for all who believe in the Lord Jesus Christ and have been baptized with water in the Name of the Father, Son and Holy Spirit.

READER 4 — It is the gate of new life and the promised Holy Spirit. We are temples of God's Spirit and have been given the gifts and fruit of the Holy Spirit to bless others and to glorify the Lord.

LEADER — If you have given your life to Jesus Christ and know Him to be your Savior and Lord, but have never paid much attention to the Holy Spirit, this might be the gate you've been looking for. I invite you to stand with me at the Fountain Gate.

If you have surrendered to Jesus Christ as your Savior and Lord and invited the Holy Spirit to be released in your life, purposing to rely upon His strength and power rather than your own, then this is your gate. If like me, you are a leaky earthen vessel in need of a fresh indwelling of the Holy Spirit, come and stand with me.

---

186   1 Corinthians 6:19

INVITATION – RESPONSE – MUSIC – PRAYER

The Leader invites people in the congregation who are lead by the Holy Spirit to stand with brothers and sister who have gathered at the Fountain Gate. Those remaining in the congregation are asked to extend their hands toward the people at the Fountain Gate.

The Leader prays for the indwelling of the Holy Spirit—

LEADER – Heavenly Father, we love you. We surrender our lives to Your Son our Savior and Lord, Jesus Christ. We empty ourselves of anything that stands in the way of receiving Your Holy Spirit. Holy Spirit, promise of Jesus, we need You. Strengthen us with Your gifts. Be abundant in Your fruitfulness.

Breathe on us breath of God, full-measure, presseddown, shaken–together, over-flowing into our laps that all we are and everything we do will be guided and empowered by the Holy Spirit to bring You glory. Amen.

(Pause)

When the prayer and ministry are finished, the Leader gives each person who has come to the Fountain Gate a prayer card with Holy Spirit art on one side and Acts 1:8, the promise of the Holy Spirit on the other.

7. WATER GATE: BIBLICAL PREACHING & TEACHING

(Power Point)

WATER GATE
Biblical Preaching & Teaching

- The Water Gate did not need repairs. God's Word is sufficient unto itself and stands forever!
- When all the walls and gates had been repaired, "...*Ezra the priest brought the Law before the assembly. He read it aloud from daybreak till noon as he faced the Water Gate in the presence of the men and women and others who could understand. And all the people listened attentively to the Book of the Law.*" **Neh 8:1-3**
- **Rom 10:17** Paul writes, "...*faith comes from hearing the message, and the message is heard through the word of Christ.*"

READER 6 – In **Neh 3:25-26** we read: *Pedaiah son of Parosh and the temple servants living on the hill of Ophel made repairs up to a point opposite the Water Gate toward the east and the projecting tower.* It is noteworthy that the Water Gate itself did not need repairs, only the walls on either side of the gate. In the Bible, water is used as a symbol of cleansing and as a metaphor for the Word of God.

READER 3 – The author of Hebrews tells us that we can *"draw near to God with a sincere heart and with the full assurance that faith brings, having our hearts sprinkled to cleanse us from a guilty conscience and having our bodies washed with pure water."* [187]

READER 5 – The gate before this was the Fountain Gate, which proclaims the outpouring of the Holy Spirit on Jesus' followers. The Fountain Gate is followed by the Water Gate, which focuses on the cleansing ministry of Holy Baptism.

READER 1 – After Nehemiah and the Israelites had repaired all the walls and gates, the Scriptures tell us that:… *on the first day of the seventh month Ezra the priest brought the Law before the assembly, which was made up of men and women and all who were able to understand. He read it aloud from daybreak till noon as he faced the square before the Water Gate in the presence of the men, women and others who could understand. And all the people listened attentively to the Book of the Law.* [188] God's Word is sufficient unto itself and stands forever!

READER 4 — In **Acts 6:2-7**, the apostles set apart as deacons seven men filled with the Holy Spirit to care for the needs of the fellowship, so that the apostles could focus on prayer and preaching. The fruit of this plan was that:… *the word of God spread. The number of disciples in Jerusalem*

187 Hebrews 10:22
188 Nehemiah 8:1-3

increased rapidly, and a large number of priests became obedient to the faith.[189]

READER 3 — Later in **Acts 19:9-12**, we read that while Paul was in Ephesus, he lead twelve disciples into the baptism of the Holy Spirit. But after preaching in the synagogue for three months, some of the people become obstinate. *So Paul left them. He took the disciples with him and had discussions daily in the lecture hall of Tyrannus. This went on for two years, so that all the Jews and Greeks who lived in the province of Asia heard the word of the Lord.*[190]

READER 2 — How many of the Jews and Greeks who lived in the province of Asia heard the Word of the Lord?

READERS 1, 3, 4 — ALL!

READER 6 – The passage continues: *God did extraordinary miracles through Paul, so that even handkerchiefs and aprons that had touched him were taken to the sick, and their illnesses were cured and the evil spirits left them.*[191]

READER 2 – Writing to the Roman believers, Paul says, *"... faith comes from hearing the message, and the message is heard through the word of Christ."*[192]

READER 3 — Peter states this same truth more poetically: *"Now that you have purified yourselves by obeying the truth so that you have sincere love for your brothers, love one another deeply, from the heart. For you have been born*

---

189   Acts 6:7
190   Acts 19:9b-10
191   Acts 19:11-12
192   Romans 10:17

again, not of perishable seed, but of imperishable, through the living and enduring word of God. For, 'All men are like grass, and all their glory is like the flowers of the field; the grass withers and the flowers fall, but the word of the Lord stands forever." [193]

LEADER — This is your gate if you are committed to read, mark, learn and inwardly digest the Scriptures on a regular basis because it is both cleansing and nourishment (milk and meat) to you. If you teach or participate in a Bible Study, home fellowship, minister in Sunday School or Vacation Bible School, this is your gate. If you are a parent who is conscientiously imparting biblical truths to your children or have been called by God to teach or preach His Word, the Water Gate is where you serve.

INVITATION – RESPONSE – MUSIC – PRAYER

The Leader invites those who stood at the Fountain Gate to place their hand on the shoulder of those who have identified the Water Gate as expressing their gifts and ministry. The congregation is asked to extend their hands toward the people at the Water Gate.

The Leader offers a prayer of thanksgiving and blessing upon them that their calling would be repeatedly confirmed, that they would be diligent in reading and studying Holy Scripture, that those principles and precepts

---

193   1 Peter 1:22-25

would be written on their hearts and evident in all they think, say and do — all to God's glory.

When the prayers are finished the Leader gives each person at the Water Gate a ribbon page marker with a Cross for their Bible.

LEADER – Next Sunday we will explore the final three gates of Nehemiah's Jerusalem: The Horse Gate; the East Gate, which after Jesus' ascension was named the Golden Gate; and the Inspection or Muster Gate.

I invite those who came to one or more of this morning's four gates to raise your hand. If you are near a person with their hand up, place your hand on their shoulder as we pray together:

(Power Point: Order of Worship)

LEADER & PEOPLE —

Heavenly Father,

We humble ourselves before You.

Thank You for calling and blessing us.

We purpose to be good stewards of the ministry gifts You give.

We will serve at the gate to which You have assigned us.

Father, please expand our spheres of influence.

Keep Your Hand upon us at all times.

Protect us from evil and harm, and from causing
    others pain.
Bless us to be a blessing to others as Your
    witnesses, ministers, and missionaries
To advance Your kingdom and bring You glory.
We ask this in Jesus' Name. Amen.

THIRD SUNDAY
REVIEW

READER 1 – Good Morning! We're returning to the Book
of Nehemiah, Chapter 3. This is the account of Nehemiah's
journey to the city of Jerusalem where he found the walls
and gates destroyed and the city in disarray.

    Before we begin, I invite you to greet your fellow trav-
elers by passing the Peace. A friendly "hey", handshake, or
embrace is appropriate, along with the words…

(Power Point: Order of Worship)

READER 1 – The Peace of Christ be with you.

PEOPLE – And also with you.

(Pause while the Peace is passed.)

(Power Point)

REVIEW
First Week
- **Sheep Gate:** Healing
- **Fish Gate:** Fishers of Men through Friendship
- **Old Gate:** Church Sacraments, History & Traditions

Second Week
- **Valley Gate:** Mercy to the poor and afflicted
- **Dung Gate:** Repentance, Confession of Sin, Forgiveness and Forgiving Others
- **Fountain Gate:** Renewal of the Holy Spirit
- **Water Gate:** Biblical Teaching & Preaching

READER 2 — The Ten Gates of Nehemiah's Jerusalem reveal the heart and passion of Jesus' ministry, a pattern for church growth, a believer's spiritual journey, and the gifts God gives believers for ministry.

READER 1 — Each Gate presents us with an **invitation** and challenges us to make a **decision**.

READER 3 — The purpose of the gates is **traffic**. In a secular city, traffic enables commerce. In the holy City of God, traffic gives opportunity for **witness, ministry** and **mission**.

READER 2 — People enter through a gate in response to the gate's purpose and the person's need. As believers identify God's call on their lives and mature in the gifts God gives them, they minister at the corresponding gate, or pass through that gate to minister in a mission field outside the City of God.

READER 4 — Each gate was established with a purpose. The past two Sundays we explored the...

(Power Point: Gates One Through Seven)

SHEEP GATE: healing in body, soul and spirit.

FISH GATE: fishers of men through friendship evangelism.

OLD GATE: Church sacraments, traditions and history.

VALLEY GATE: mercy to those in crisis, the poor, rejected, abused and grieving.

DUNG or REFUSE GATE: confession of sin with repentance, forgiveness, and forgiving others.

FOUNTAIN GATE: ministry in the power of the Holy Spirit.

WATER GATE: Biblical preaching and teaching.

LEADER — If you were here the past two Sundays and came forward to stand at a gate, please raise your hand.

Wow! Praise God! Some of you may have gone to more than one gate. I invite you to stand at the gate that has the greatest impact in your life.

The Leader invites people to the gates as a refresher and to model a response to the coming invitations. The Leader invites the congregation to extend their hands toward those at the gates and prays a blessing on the people standing at the gates before they return to their seats.

READER 4 – Nehemiah is a leader of God's people. He teaches us three lessons about leadership.
Influence is the true measure of leadership.
Leaders are **lifelong learners**.
Trust is the foundation of leadership. When a leader breaks trust, the capacity to lead is forfeited. Nehemiah's leadership bears witness to these principles.

READER 5 – Jerusalem is a metaphor for the City of God: outside is the darkness that shrouds the world; inside the walls and gates, there is the light of God's presence.

READER 6 – Jesus' friend Lazarus grew very sick. Mary and Martha, Lazarus' sisters, turned to Jesus for help. They had seen His miracles.

READER 5 – Any difficult circumstance we face can ultimately bring glory to God because God can bring good out of any bad situation.

READER 6 – Lazarus died and his body was placed in a dark tomb, where it lay decaying for four days. Moved with deep emotion and weeping, Jesus had the stone rolled away from the tomb. He prayed and then commanded in a loud voice, *"Lazarus, come out!" The dead man came out, his hands and feet wrapped with strips of linen, and a* *cloth around his face. Jesus said to them, "Take off the grave clothes and let him go."* [194]

READER 3 — Darkness to Light; Sickness to Health; Death to Eternal Life; Bondage to Freedom; Isolation to Friendship – Lazarus experienced all this and more when Jesus raised him from the dead. Lazarus' resurrection prefigures Jesus' resurrection and the victorious, eternal life Jesus has secured for those who accept Him as Savior and Lord.

READER 4 — Outside the gates of the City of God are darkness, sickness, death, bondage and isolation. Inside the gates are light, the fullness of life now and eternally, freedom from sin, and friendship in the presence of God.

READER 2 – Today we will explore the last three gates: the **Horse Gate**, the **East Gate**, and the **Muster Gate**. These gates are prophetic in that each proclaims the second coming of Jesus Christ. The Horse Gate's prophetic message is found in the Book of Revelation which tells us that on the day of Jesus' return, Heaven will stand open and He will appear on a white horse with all the fury of the wrath of God Almighty.[195] God set aside the East Gate for the sole purpose of Jesus the Messiah's eventual return to Jerusalem.[196] The Muster Gate prefigures the Judgment Seat of Christ.[197]

READER 1 — The Gates cry out to everyone with Jesus' invitation, *"Come to me, all you who are weary and burdened,*

194   John 11:43-44
195   Revelation 19:11-15
196   Ezekiel 44:1-3
197   Matthew 25:312 & 2 Corinthians 5:10

and I will give you rest. Take my yoke upon you and learn from me, for I am gentle and humble in heart, and you will find rest for your souls. For my yoke is easy and my burden is light." [198]

READER 4 – Lets explore the last three gates.

8. HORSE GATE: SPIRITUAL WARFARE

(Power Point)

HORSE GATE
Spiritual Warfare

- Paul teaches the vital principles of spiritual warfare and deliverance in **2 Corinthians** and **Ephesians**
- There is no neutral ground; spiritual warfare is not an option. **1 Peter 5:8-9** & **1 John 4:4**
- One third of Jesus' ministry was focused on spiritual warfare. With confidence we can say with Paul, "*...thanks be to God! He gives us the victory through our lord Jesus Christ.*" **1 Cor 15:26**
- We can clothe ourselves in the full armor of God. **Eph 6:10-18**

READER 1 – In **Neh 3:28** we read that: *Above the Horse Gate, the priests made repairs, each in front of his own*

---

198   Matthew 11:28-30

house. Horses were not allowed inside the city walls. This was the gate where they were tethered, fed and watered.

READER 4 – Horses require a great deal of grazing land and water; both were precious commodities in Israel. As a result, horses were never abundant in Israel's history. David and Solomon were the exception. They developed a cavalry of twelve thousand horsemen and fourteen hundred chariots. Horses were primarily instruments of war, valued for strength and swiftness. For most of Israel's history their enemies entered the field of battle with larger, better equipped armies, leading David to write: *Some trust in chariots and some in horses, but we trust in the name of the Lord our God.*[199] *A horse is a vain hope for deliverance; despite all its great strength it cannot save.*[200]

READER 2 – The Horse Gate is all about warfare. Whether we know it or not, ever since the Fall, humanity has been daily engaged in spiritual warfare.

READER 3 – As a young man, Paul served as a Roman soldier. He applied what he learned in the military to his service of the Lord, teaching the Church vital principles of spiritual warfare.

Paul identifies the enemy:... *our struggle is not against flesh and blood, but against the rulers, against the authorities, against the powers of this dark world and against the spiritual forces of evil in heavenly realms.*[201]

---

199   Psalm 20: 7
200   Psalm 33:17
201   Ephesians 6:12

Paul reveals the Church's strategy: *"For though we live in the world, we do not wage war as the world does. The weapons we fight with are not the weapons of the world. On the contrary, they have divine power to demolish arguments and every pretension that sets itself up against the knowledge of God, and we take captive every thought to make it obedient to Christ."* [202]

READER 1 — Paul inventories the weapons we bring to the warfare:

"Therefore put on the full armor of God, so that when the day of evil comes, you may be able to stand your ground, and after you have done everything, to stand. Stand firm then, with the belt of truth buckled around your waist, with the breastplate of righteousness in place, and with your feet fitted with the readiness that comes from the gospel of peace. In addition to all this, take up the shield of faith, with which you can extinguish all the flaming arrows of the evil one. Take the helmet of salvation and the sword of the Spirit, which is the word of God. And pray in the Spirit on all occasions with all kinds of prayers and requests. With this in mind, be alert and always keep on praying for all the Lord's people.[203]

READER 4 – Jesus equips His disciples for spiritual warfare with a two-word strategy (bind and loose) and one weapon (authority). In the Gospel of Matthew, He tells the disciples: *"I will give you the keys of the kingdom of heaven; whatever you bind on earth will be bound in heaven, and whatever you loose on earth will be loosed in heaven.*[204]

202   2 Corinthians 10:3-5
203   Ephesians 6:13-18
204   Matthew 16:19

Jesus repeated this promise to emphasize its importance: *Truly I tell you, whatever you bind on earth will be bound in heaven, and whatever you loose on earth will be loosed in heaven.*[205]

As we carry forward the ministry of Jesus in the midst of spiritual warfare, we are given the authority to bind ourselves to the things of God, and loose ourselves from the things of the devil. We are to do the same for people who allow us to pray for them. Binding and loosing are an important part of ministry.

READER 3 – We live in a war zone. There is no neutral ground. Spiritual warfare is not optional. We can let Satan and his demons have their way, or we can learn to resist, fight, and be victorious sharing in the Victory that Jesus Christ won for us.

Peter warns us: *Your enemy the devil prowls around like a roaring lion looking for someone to devour. Resist him, standing firm in the faith. . ..*[206]

John encourages us to remember our identity, *"You, dear children, are from God and have overcome them, because the one who is in you is greater than the one who is in the world."*[207]

READER 2 – Spiritual warfare is not without a redemptive purpose in God's plan. It perpetuates the ministry of Jesus as prophesied by Isaiah,[208] and destroys the works of the devil.[209]

---

205   Matthew 18:18
206   1 Peter 5:8-9
207   1 John 4:4
208   Isaiah 61:1-4 & Luke 4:18-19
209   1 John 3:8

Spiritual warfare refines believers through trials by fire, promoting growth and maturity. Jesus increases and we decrease.[210] Paul outlines this process in his letter to the Romans:... *we also glory in our sufferings, because we know that suffering produces perseverance; perseverance, character; and character, hope. And hope does not put to shame, because God's love has been poured out into our hearts through the Holy Spirit, who has been given to us.*[211] Spiritual warfare brings glory to Christ who *"is all, and is in all"*[212]

READER 1 – Jesus waged war with Satan in the wilderness in preparation for public ministry and victoriously at His death upon the Cross. A third of Jesus' ministry focused on loosing people from the grip of demons and binding people to the Good News of salvation. Along with Paul, we can say with confidence: *"... thanks be to God! He gives us the victory through our Lord Jesus Christ."*[213]

READER 4 — The Horse Gate is also prophetic, declaring the end time judgment and return of Jesus Christ! Listen to what John records in the Book of Revelation: *I saw heaven standing open and there before me was a white horse, whose rider is called Faithful and True. With justice he judges and wages war.*[214]

READER 3 – Paul tells us how to prepare for that time:... *you know very well that the day of the Lord will come like*

---

210   John 3:30
211   Romans 5:3-5
212   Colossians 3:11
213   1 Corinthians 15:57
214   Revelation 19:11

a thief in the night.... But you, brothers and sisters, are not in darkness so that this day should surprise you like a thief. You are all children of the light and children of the day. We do not belong to the night or to the darkness. So then, let us not be like others, who are asleep, but let us be awake and sober.... . putting on faith and love as a breastplate, and the hope of salvation as a helmet. For God did not appoint us to suffer wrath but to receive salvation through our Lord Jesus Christ.[215]

LEADER — Spiritual warfare requires obedience, discipline, and perseverance, along with the unity of the Church. This is not a "Lone Ranger" ministry. It is a *"two or three gather in my* (Jesus') *name, there am I with them"*[216] ministry. If you have a passion to see the captives set free in the Victory of Jesus, the Horse Gate may be your assignment. If you are an intercessor or are seen by others to be a prayer warrior, this is your gate. If the Lord has given you the ability to see things as they are and speak truth in love, this is where you belong.

INVITATION – RESPONSE – MUSIC – PRAYER

The Leader invites those who last week stood at the Water Gate to place their hand on the shoulder of those brothers and sister who have identified the Horse Gate as expressing their gifts and ministry. The congregation

215 1 Thessalonians 5:2, 4-6, 8b-9
216 Matthew 18:20 (addition mine)

is asked to extend their hands toward the people at the Horse Gate.

The Leader offers a prayer of thanksgiving and blessing upon them that their calling would be repeatedly confirmed, that they be clothed in the full armor of God, that they remain constant in prayer, knowing the Holy Spirit as their constant guide, and that they would see strongholds destroyed in the Victory of Jesus Christ – all to God's glory.

When the prayers are completed the Leader gives each person at the Horse Gate a Pocket Crucifix.

9. GOLDEN or EAST GATE: THE PRESENCE OF GOD

(Power Point)

GOLDEN or EAST GATE
The Presence of God

- Many people believe this is the gate through which the Messiah will return. It leads directly into the Holy of Holies.
- Paul assures us **in Eph 2:5** that, *"God raised us up with Christ and seated us with him in the heavenly realms in Christ Jesus."*

READER 1 – In **Nehemiah 3:29-30**, we read: *Next to them, Zadok son of Immer made repairs opposite his house. Next to him, Shemaiah son of Shekaniah, the guard at the East Gate, made repairs. Next to him, Hananiah son of Shelemiah, and Hanun, the sixth son of Zalaph, repaired another section. Next to them, Meshullam son of Berekiah made repairs opposite his living quarters.*

READER 2 — The East Gate opened onto the Temple Mount and faced directly across the Kidron Valley from the Mount of Olives and Garden of Gethsemane, where Jesus and His disciples prayed before He was betrayed and arrested.

READER 3 — This is the gate through which many believe the Messiah will return, for it is the gate that leads directly to the Holy of Holies. This is where God's throne — the Mercy Seat — is located in the Temple. As a result the East Gate has been renamed the Golden Gate. It is the gate of awe in the presence of the Lord. It is also the only gate that has been mortared closed with stone.

READER 4 — The prophet Ezekiel gives a startling account of entering the throne room of God through the East or Golden Gate: *Then the man brought me to the gate facing east, and I saw the glory of the God of Israel coming from the east. His voice was like the roar of rushing waters, and the land was radiant with his glory. . . I fell facedown. The glory of the LORD entered the temple through the gate facing east. Then the Spirit lifted me up and brought me into the inner court, and the glory of the LORD filled the temple. While the man was standing beside me, I heard someone speaking to* *me from inside the temple. He said: "Son of man, this is the place of my throne and the place for the soles of my feet."* [217]

READER 3 — Paul assures us: *God raised us up with Christ and seated us with him in the heavenly realms in Christ Jesus...* [218] In the Temple, the presence of the Lord is in the Holy of Holies where we are seated with Christ Jesus between the wings of the Cherubim.

READER 1 – The Horse Gate told us that we are in a constant state of spiritual warfare and reminded us of Jesus' promised return. The East Gate has a similar message because God is serious about our living our lives not only in the moment, but also with eternity in mind.

READER 2 — Jesus promised we would become living stones and temples of His Holy Spirit. His promise was fulfilled at Pentecost. The indwelling of the Holy Spirit within every believer makes us bearers of God's presence.

LEADER – This is the gate where Christians lay aside their divisions and come together. There is One Church of Jesus Christ comprised of many congregations. At the Golden Gate we experience unity that enables us to pray for and serve in the city where we live or in far away mission fields.

You came through the East or Golden Gate this morning. Do you know that? It is the Sunday Gate, the entrance to worship. It is the "Jesus is here" gate that welcomes us into His transforming presence. The East or Golden Gate is like the Temple Veil that was torn from top to bottom

---

217   Ezekiel 43:1-7
218   Ephesians 2:6

by the hand of God when Jesus died on Calvary's Cross –
giving all believers access to the Holy of Holies.

(Power Point: Order of Worship)

LEADER – Jesus is here!

PEOPLE – Alleluia, Jesus is here.

LEADER & PEOPLE –

Holy, holy, holy Lord, God of power and might
Heaven and earth are full of Your glory.
Hosanna in the highest.
Blessed is He who comes in the name of the Lord.
Hosanna In the highest. *(Sanctus may be sung.)*

LEADER – Since we have entered into the Lord's presence in Sunday worship, let's express our unity by forming groups of three or four to pray God's blessing on one another.

Once the people have formed small groups, the Leader prays for all to know the presence of God and invites them to start praying for one another. The prayers can go on for ten minutes. After about eight minutes the Leader encourages people to come to a close. The Leader then ends the prayer time with a blessing.

The Leader gives everyone a prayer card with a picture of the glorified Christ on one side and the passage from John 17:20b-23a on the other side. It is a gift to remind us all that as believers in Jesus Christ we stand together at the Golden Gate.

10. MUSTER or INSPECTION GATE: HOLINESS OF LIFE

(Power Point)

MUSTER or INSPECTION GATE
Holiness of Life

- **Obedience** & **Accountability** enable us to conform to the Kingdom of God, not the world.
- **1 John 4:18** tells how we are to do this. God's perfect love overcomes our fears. We are perfected in God's love as we surrender to Him.
- At the Inspection Gate, it is not our work that is being evaluated; it is our stewardship of God's work in and through us.
- **Matt 13:45-46 & 1 Peter 2:9-10**

READER 3 – The last gate. In **Nehemiah 3:31-32**, we read: *Next to him, Malkijah, one of the goldsmiths, made repairs as far as the house of the temple servants and the merchants, opposite the Inspection Gate, and as far as the room above the corner; and between the room above the corner and the Sheep Gate the goldsmiths and merchants made repairs.*

READER 2 — This is the gate of accountability. Peter writes: *As obedient children, do not conform to the evil desires you had when you lived in ignorance. But just as he who called you is holy, so be holy in all you do. For it is written: "Be holy, because I am holy."* [219]

READER 1 – Sometimes we must leave all that's familiar and risk everything in search of something precious and of inestimable value. Jesus said: *". . . the kingdom of heaven is like a merchant looking for fine pearls. When he found one of great value, he went away and sold everything he had and bought it."* [220] Holiness is the *"pearl of great price"* for which we would be willing to sell everything. Holiness is total surrender to an intimate relationship with God.

READER 4 — Holiness and perfection are very similar to one another. Jesus commands us to: *"Be perfect, therefore, as your heavenly Father is perfect."* [221]

READER 1 – John reveals how we are to fulfill this command, *"There is no fear in love. But perfect love drives out fear, because fear has to do with punishment. The one who fears is not made perfect in love."* [222]

READER 3 — God's perfect love for us not only overcomes our fears, His love perfects us as we surrender to Him and allow Him to work in and through us. The burden of perfection and holiness is not upon us, but upon Him. The question for us is, will we cooperate and yield to His inspection? Advent and Lent are times set aside in the Christian Calendar for inspection or muster.

---

219   1 Peter 1:14-16
220   Matthew 13:45-46
221   Matthew 5:48
222   1 John 4:18

READER 4 – Muster is a formal military term used for the act of assembling for inspection. The ultimate inspection is the Judgment Seat of Christ. We are told in the Gospel of Matthew that: *"When the Son of Man comes in his glory, and all the angels with him, he will sit on his glorious throne. All the nations will be gathered before him, and he will separate the people one from another as a shepherd separates the sheep from the goats."* [223]

READER 2 – Here's what happens to the sheep: *"Then the King will say to those on his right, 'Come, you who are blessed by my Father; take your inheritance, the kingdom prepared for you since the creation of the world.'"* [224]

Listen carefully to what happens to the goats: *"Then he will say to those on his left, 'Depart from me, you who are cursed, into the eternal fire prepared for the devil and his angels.'"* [225]

God fervently desires that you and I be sheep. That is why He sent His only begotten Son, our Good Shepherd, to redeem us. *"The Lord is… patient with you, not wanting anyone to perish, but everyone to come to repentance."* [226]

READER 2 — When we pass through the Muster Gate, it is not our work that is being evaluated; it is our stewardship of God's work, accomplished through us, that has to pass muster. In response to His saving grace have we acted on the things He has called us to do?

---

223 Matthew 25:31-32
224 Matthew 25:34
225 Matthew 25:41
226 2 Peter 3:9

READER 3 — 1 Peter 2:9-10 reassures us of our identity:… *you are a chosen people, a royal priesthood, a holy nation, a people belonging to God, that you may declare the praises of him who called you out of darkness into his wonderful light. Once you were not a people, but now you are the people of God; once you had not received mercy, but now you have received mercy.*

LEADER – The Muster Gate is for all believers who have learned to stand before Jesus Christ for regular inspection, to be held accountable, to receive orders, and to be blessed by Him as we serve His Church, advancing His Kingdom.

It is my hope and prayer that every one of us desires to grow in holiness, but before I pray for everyone here, I want you to look around. If there is a person in whom you identify holiness, whose life encourages you to grow in holiness, make a mental note and express your appreciation to them before you go home.

While I pray for all of us at the Muster Gate to grow in holiness, I invite you to put your hand over your heart.

The Leader prays that we will be attentive to the Holy Spirit, that we will see our need for holiness, that we will understand and conform to Jesus Christ, that we will identify areas of sin and repent, that we will allow brothers and sisters in Christ to hold us accountable, that we will live by the Bible's principles and precepts in the grace and strength of the Holy Spirit.
The Leader gives everyone at the gate a prayer card with a picture of a church on one side and 1 Peter 2:9-10

on the other as a reminder that at the Muster Gate we are held accountable as ambassadors for God's kingdom.

LEADER – We've covered a lot of ground together these past few Sundays exploring the ten gates of Jerusalem in the days of Nehemiah. It's been like a pilgrimage to the Holy City of God. Let's take a moment to summarize and review what we've learned.

(Power Point)

REVIEW: Ten Gates of Nehemiah's Jerusalem

- **Sheep Gate:** Healing
- **Fish Gate:** Fishers of Men through Friendship
- **Old Gate:** Church Sacraments, History & Traditions
- **Valley Gate:** Mercy to those in Crisis, the Poor, Rejected, Abused and Grieving
- **Dung Gate:** Repentance, Confession of Sin, Forgiveness, Forgiving Others
- **Fountain Gate:** Renewal of the Holy Spirit
- **Water Gate:** Biblical Preaching and Teaching
- **Horse Gate:** Spiritual Warfare and Deliverance
- **Golden or East Gate:** Presence of God
- **Muster Gate:** Holiness of Life

READER 1 – The Sheep Gate represents our salvation through Jesus' Cross and Resurrection.

READER 2 – The Fish Gate reminds us that we are all on mission for Jesus Christ, whether in the city where we live or some far away place. All of us are called to be evangelists by being prepared to witness to our faith in Jesus Christ and share our testimony.

READER 3 – The Old Gate signifies our instruction in God's ancient truth through Holy Scripture and Church traditions. God's truth is also revealed in nature, history, art and science.

READER 4 – The Valley Gate addresses the trials and tests of life that shape our character to reflect Jesus' love and mercy.

READER 5 – The Dung Gate is a call to repentance, confession of sin, asking forgiveness from God, and forgiving those who have sinned against us. It's the place to quickly dump your garbage.

READER 6 – The Fountain Gate represents the spring of living water that came on Pentecost with the outpouring of the Holy Spirit.

READER 5 – The Water Gate represents God's cleansing through the word of God and His encouragement to live holy lives.

READER 4 – The Horse Gate calls us to vigilance for we live in a fallen world and are in a state of spiritual warfare.

READER 3 – The East Gate welcomes us into God's transforming presence in worship and reminds us to be ever ready for the return of Jesus Christ.

READER 2 – The Muster Gate holds us accountable now and reminds us that one day we will stand before the Judgment Seat of Christ for our final inspection where we will want to be counted with the sheep and not the goats. The Muster Gate encourages us to live our daily lives with Eternity in mind.

READER 1 – Whether we are entering the city to worship God and find rest and refreshment in His presence or are leaving the city on a mission, all ten gates call out to us with strong encouragement: *"Therefore we also, since we are surrounded by so great a cloud of witnesses, let us lay aside every weight, and the sin which so easily ensnares us, and let us run with endurance the race that is set before us, looking unto Jesus, the author and finisher of our faith, who for the joy that was set before Him endured the cross, despising the shame, and has sat down at the right hand of the throne of God."* [227]

LEADER – I pray that during our journey around the holy city you've come to understand more about yourself and your brothers and sisters in Christ. My hope is that you've seen Jesus, and come to know more of His call upon your life, the gifts of the Holy Spirit entrusted to you, and the ministry and mission to which you've been called.

I invite those who came to one or more of this morning's three gates to raise their hand. If you are near a person

---

227   Hebrews 12:1-2 **New King James Version**

with their hand up, place your hand on their shoulder as we pray together:

(Power Point: Order of Worship)

LEADER & PEOPLE —

Heavenly Father,

We humble ourselves before You.

Thank You for calling and blessing us.

We purpose to be good stewards of the ministry gifts You give.

We will serve at the gate to which You have assigned us.

Father, please expand our spheres of influence.

Keep Your Hand upon us at all times.

Keep us from temptation and protect us from evil.

Bless us to be a blessing to others

As Your royal priesthood may we advance Your kingdom
and bring You glory.

We ask this in Jesus' Name. Amen.

Second Script

THE TABERNACLE:
GOD'S PORTRAIT OF JESUS CHRIST

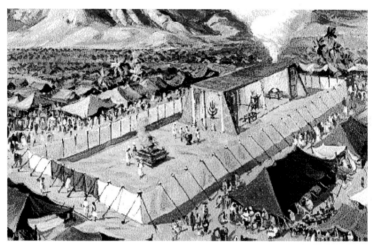

228

History and Glossary

Christ the King Church was loaned a meticulously constructed model of the wilderness Tabernacle. God had commanded Moses to build the Tabernacle as a place for His presence with His people after their exodus from 400 years of slavery in Egypt. The model was eight feet long and four feet wide. It was placed in the church vestibule where people entering and exiting worship would

---

228   Purchased artist's rendering of the Tabernacle use in the Power Point presentations.

encounter it. The congregation's response to the model was disconcerting.

"Interesting. The guy put a lot of work into it, but I don't get it."

"What's it about?"

"I read about the Tabernacle in my Bible, but I still don't understand where it fits into the whole picture."

"What's that tent thing have to do with Jesus?"

This script is the response to the congregation's need for instruction, plus an opportunity to experience invitational and interactive worship.

For forty years, I've been an Anglican who is both sacramental and liturgical. I understand that much of the wider Church is not. I hope this glossary of terms, set forth in the order of their appearance in the script, is helpful:

Acolyte – someone (usually a young person) who helps the person leading worship.

Alb – a white ankle length robe.

Cruet - a small flat-bottomed vessel with a narrow neck and stopper, used to hold water, wine, or oil.

Lavabo – the ceremony and the bowl for the celebrant washing hands after receiving the offering.

Aspergillum – a small-perforated container with a handle that is used for sprinkling Holy Water as a reminder of baptism.

Holy Water – water that has been blessed.

Laver - a large basin used for ceremonial washing in the Tabernacle. It has become the Baptismal Font in Christian congregations and may also be a bowl for hand and foot washing.

Golden Lamp Stand – a Jewish menorah or candelabra that holds seven candles.

Table of Shewbread – In some Christian congregations this has become the Credence Table situated on the right (epistle) side of the Altar or Communion Table. It holds the bread, water and wine for the Lord's Supper.

Altar of Incense – in the Tabernacle this was called the Golden Altar. In today's churches, it has become the **Thurible**, a metal censor suspended from three chains in which incense is burned during worship. It represents prayers of the people rising to God.

Torches – candles attached to wooden poles, most often carried by acolytes.

Paschal, Easter, or Christ Candle – a large white candle that is blessed and lit every year at Easter. It is used through the Easter Season, and throughout the year on special occasions like baptisms and funerals.

Holy Oil – a blessed and perfumed oil representing the presence and power of the Holy Spirit.[229]

Ciborium – a small lidded container for holding the communion bread.

---

229   Exodus 29:7 & 31:11

Paten – a plate used to carry the communion bread.

Stole   - a liturgical vestment denoting the yoke of Christ.

Chasuble – outer most vestment worn by some clergy to celebrate the Lord's Supper, similar to the Tabernacle High Priest's Ephod.

Sanctus Bells – originally the bells were attached to the hem of the High Priest's robes. Today some Christian congregations use Sanctus Bells to create a joyful noise to the Lord as they give thanks for the amazing grace of the Lord's Supper.

SCRIPT

Taped on the floor is the outline of the Tabernacle of Moses. Inside the perimeter are outlines of the Outer Court, Holy Place, and Holy of Holies. The congregation is seated at the Entrance and along two sides of the Outer Court. The music ministry is on one side of the Holy of Holies. The Veil of the Holy of Holies is closed, keeping the Ark of the Covenant, Pillar of cloud and fire, and Cherubim from the congregation's view.

Tabernacle Complex

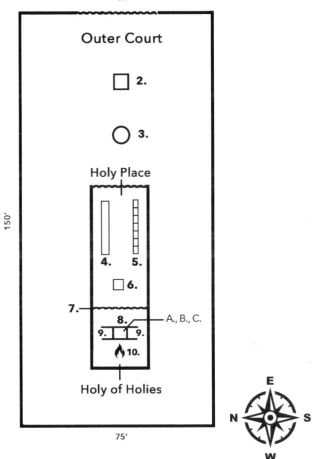

1. Entrance,
2. Brazen Altar
3. Laver
4. Table of Shewbread
5. Golden Lamp Stand
6. Golden Altar or Altar of Incense
7. Veil

8. Ark of the Covenant
   Contents of the Ark
   A. Ten Commandments
   B. Aaron's Staff
   C. Unspoiled Manna
9. Two Cherubim
10. Pillar of Fire and Cloud

For a large worship space the presentation team consists of the Leader (often a pastor)*, two assistants, two acolytes, six script readers* (best recruited from the Youth Group)*, the Music Ministry, sound and projection engineers, a Setup Team of four people to build the set during the presentation, and four teams of two* (male & female) *for prayer and ministry to people responding to the invitations. Instructions are in italicized bold print.*

The Leader is the presenter of the entire experience. Although the part is totally scripted, the Leader's impromptu offerings are essential to the flow of the presentation. The Leader is dressed in an alb, cincture, and sandals much like the ancient Hebrews.

Ideally, each part of the Tabernacle is identified with a sign naming the feature and in some cases stating its Old and New Testament significance. In addition, Power-Point projections help illustrate the elements and progress of the Tabernacle worship, as well as the congregational responses and music lyrics.

The presentation should last 1 ¾ to 2 hours with time afterward for ministry and fellowship. Rehearsals are held as needed to prepare for the presentation.

INTRODUCTION

READER 1 – Welcome. You are about to step into a "Time Machine." We will travel back to 1450 B.C. when God instructed Moses to build a Tabernacle so that He could dwell with His people during their time in the wilderness following four centuries of slavery. The Tabernacle is God's dwelling place with His people. In Jesus we become God's tabernacle.

During our journey we will see how the Tabernacle has influenced the Church today. Church architecture, furniture, and fundamental aspects of worship find their roots in the wilderness Tabernacle, which is a prophecy fulfilled in Jesus Christ.

Before we begin, I invite you to greet your fellow travelers by passing the Peace of Christ. A friendly "hey", handshake, or embrace is appropriate, along with the words...

(Power Point: Order of Worship)

LEADER – The Peace of Jesus Christ be with you.

PEOPLE – And also with you.

READER 2 – Please greet one another.

(Pause while the Peace is passed.)

(Power Point)

Purpose of the Tabernacle

- God's dwelling place with his people
- In Jesus we become God's tabernacle

READER 5 – The diagram on the floor shows us how the Tabernacle was laid out. As we explore this ancient Hebrew place of worship, we will discover that it reveals a prophecy fulfilled, a pattern for worship, the way of salvation, a portrait of Jesus, and a picture of you and me.

Today's leader is_____.
Our leader plays the role of the high priest. All the people assisting in the presentation represent members of the tribe of Levi who cared for the Tabernacle and conducted the worship that occurred there.

READER 4 – The Bible is the only book God anointed to reveal the way of salvation, the forgiveness of sin, and the promise of eternal life. It is the only book God blessed to bring hearts, minds and lives into alignment with God's will and to transform the lives of believers to reveal Jesus Christ.

Before the Bible, even before the compilation of the Torah (the first five books of the Old Testament), there were the Ten Commandments and the design for the Tabernacle, which God revealed to Moses on Mount Sinai.

READER 2 – The prophet Amos wrote what he heard from God: *"The days are coming when I will send a famine through the land – not for food or water, but a famine of hearing the words of the Lord."* [230]

Moses' task was to lead the people in hearing God's word and in worshiping Him. Pharaoh's sin was in preventing the Israelites from worshiping God. God instructed Moses to build the Tabernacle in the wilderness. The

---

230   Amos 8:11

purpose of the Tabernacle was for God's presence and communication with His people.

The word "tabernacle" means, "tent," "place of dwelling," or "sanctuary." During forty years of desert wandering, the Tabernacle was at the center of this nomadic community numbering two to three million people.

READER 1 – Before the construction of the Tabernacle, Moses erected a tent outside the encampment of Israel where God met with him. It was called the *"tent of meeting."* The pillar of cloud by day and fire by night came down and stayed at the entrance to the tent when the Lord spoke to Moses.[231]

READER 6 – After the Tabernacle was constructed and furnished, the twelve tribes pitched their tents around it according to tribal order. Those of you seated around the perimeter of the Tabernacle represent the twelve tribes of Israel. The Levites did not have a tribal area; they were assigned to live among the other tribes. Their special responsibility was for the care and transport of the Tabernacle and the worship that took place in it.[232]

READER 5 – The whole wilderness encampment, with the Tabernacle at the center and the tribes surrounding it, is a prophetic picture of today's church. It was the place where people gathered to offer sacrifice and worship. It was where God frequently met with Moses and once a year with the high priest on the Day of Atonement. In Scripture, the Holy

---

231   Exodus 33:7-11
232   Numbers 2:2, 3:7-10 & 31-34

Place and the Holy of Holies together are often referred to as the Sanctuary.

READER 3 – Tabernacle worship in the presence of God engaged people in body, soul and spirit. The worship stimulated all their senses: sight, hearing, taste, touch and smell. God created the human body with five senses. We use all five senses to communicate with one another. Likewise, God communicates with us through all our senses. The worship we render God should be an offering of *all* we are.

READER 2 – You mean, we are to put our whole self into worship, not just our soul, but our bodies and spirits as well?

READERS 1, 3 & 6 – Yes!

READER 1 – Psalm 34 suggests that we: *Taste and see that the Lord is good.*[233]

The Apostle Paul reasoned: *"If the whole body were an eye, where would the sense of hearing be? If the whole body were an ear, where would the sense of smell be?"*[234]

Hearing is what plants the seed of faith. Seeing causes our faith to mature and become fruitful. In a crisis of faith, Thomas said to the other disciples who had already been with the resurrected Lord Jesus: *"Unless I see the nail marks in his hands and put my fingers where the nails were, and put my hand into his side, I will not believe."*[235] When Jesus next meets Thomas, He invites him to touch His nail

---

233   Psalm 34:8
234   1 Corinthians 12:17
235   John 20:25

pierced hands and the spear wound in His side. Then Jesus urges Thomas to believe.

READER 3 – When we see the nature and character of God, we can better understand and worship Him. The pattern of worship God revealed to Moses engaged every aspect of who we are and enabled worshipers to experience the fearsome majesty of God, giving Him praise, honor and glory.

READER 4 – The importance of sight and sound are evident in the Gospel of Mark: *Then the disciples went out and preached everywhere...*

READER 2 – That's auditory.

READER 4 –*... and the Lord worked with them and confirmed his word by the signs that accompanied it.*[236]

READER 2 – That's visual.

READER 5 – Let's look to see how God made Himself known in the Tabernacle and it's worship. What do you think is the most exciting place on earth?

READER 1 – Any of the Seven Wonders of the World!

READER 6 – Yosemite National Park or Niagara Falls!

READER 4 – Disneyland!

READER 5 – All those places are amazing, but the Tabernacle of God was even more exciting in appearance and activity! The guiding presence of God appeared as a pillar

---

236   Mark 16:20-23

of cloud by day and a pillar of fire by night over the Holy of Holies. Life and death, blood and sacrifice, praise and worship, judgment and forgiveness, grace and mercy accosted the senses. It was both frightening and exhilarating beyond imagination.

(Power Point)

**Holy God, Sinful Man,
And the Way of Salvation**

- Jesus is the Way
- Jesus is the Truth
- Jesus is the Life

READER 6 – In the design, materials, furnishings, and worship of the Tabernacle we will find a vivid portrait of the Messiah yet to come.

READER 5 – We will discover that Jesus is here.

READER 4 – We will learn what and who we are, where we came from, and to whom we belong.

READER 3 – We will participate in God's pattern for worship, as it is fulfilled in Jesus Christ and evident in every aspect of church worship today.

READER 2 – Let us bring our body's five senses; our soul's intellect, emotions and will; and our spirits that are indwelt by the Holy Spirit to full ATTENTION as we prepare to enter the Tabernacle.

Setup Team: Diagram of the Tabernacle is placed on an easel so it can be seen throughout the presentation.

ENTRANCE

The Leader enters the Tabernacle through the only Entrance/Exit.

(Power Point)

Entrance
Only one entrance to the Tabernacle

- Only one way by which we leave the world and enter the Holy
- **Psalm 100:4** *"Enter his gates with thanksgiving and his courts with praise; give thanks to him and praise his name."*

READER 1 – There is only one Entrance to the Tabernacle– only one way by which we leave the world and enter the Holy. The order of the furniture in the Tabernacle maps the process of our salvation and sanctification.

Sunday worship begins when we enter the worship space. It involves a greeting at the door, the assistance of ushers, private devotions, hymns, possibly a processional, songs of praise, a welcome (often from Holy Scripture), and prayers.

The following words are familiar elements of our entrance into worship and the presence of God.

(Power Point: Order of Worship)

LEADER – Blessed be God: Father, Son, and Holy Spirit.

PEOPLE – And blessed be His kingdom, now and forever.

LEADER – Jesus is here!

PEOPLE – Alleluia, Jesus is here. Alleluia!

LEADER – "Almighty God, to You all hearts are open, all desires known, and from whom no secrets are hid: Cleanse the thoughts of our hearts by the inspiration of Your Holy Spirit, that we may perfectly love You and worthily magnify Your holy Name; through Jesus Christ our Lord. Amen." [237]

READER 6 – **Psalm 100** instructs us to: *Enter his gates with thanksgiving and his courts with praise; give thanks to him and praise his name.*[238]

MUSIC – FAMILIAR PRAISE SONGS
(Power-Point: Lyrics)

---

237 **1979 Book of Common Prayer**, page 355
238 Psalm 100:4

PURPOSE OF THE TABERNACLE

(Power Point)

The Tabernacle: A Pattern
For Private and Corporate Worship

God instructed Moses: *"See that you make all things according to the pattern which was shown you on the mountain."* **Exodus 25:40** [239]

- In the desert the Tabernacle is the center of worship
- In the Promised Land the Tabernacle is replaced by the Temple

---

READER 2 – The Tabernacle is God's dwelling place with His people. The book of Exodus records that God first gave building instructions to Moses in the wilderness: *"Make this tabernacle and all its furnishings exactly like the pattern I will show you."* [240] Moses passed these detailed orders concerning the Tabernacle's construction and use on to the Israelites.

God further promised: *"Then I will dwell among the Israelites and be their God. They will know that I am the Lord their God, who brought them out of Egypt so that I might dwell among them. I am the Lord their God."* [241]

Remember, God appeared among them over the Tabernacle's Holy of Holies as a pillar of cloud and fire. The

---

239   Exodus 25:40
240   Exodus 25:9
241   Exodus 29:45-46

people did not break camp and move until the pillar lifted. It was a powerful visual statement of God's presence and leadership.

READER 4 – In the New Covenant, through faith in Jesus Christ, every believer becomes a tabernacle of God. The Holy Spirit dwells, not just with us, but is present in us. Paul tells us: *"... do you not know that your bodies are temples of the Holy Spirit who is in you, whom you have received from God. You are not your own..."*[242]

READER 5 – Jesus said: *And I will ask the Father, and he will give you another advocate to help you and be with you forever— the Spirit of truth. The world cannot accept him, because it neither sees him nor knows him. But you know him, for he lives with you and will be in you. I will not leave you as orphans; I will come to you."*[243] Our lives are to be filled with and guided by the Holy Spirit, who tabernacles with us.

READER 1 – In the Tabernacle we encounter all three persons of the Holy Trinity: God the Father; God the only begotten Son, Jesus Christ; and God the Holy Spirit.

READER 3 – A fence establishes the boundary of the Outer Court. Inside the fence is the Tabernacle or Tent of Meeting. As we enter the Outer Court to worship God, the first piece of furniture we encounter is the Brazen Altar where animals were sacrificed.

God and sinners meet at the Brazen Altar. It is a prophetic representation of Christ who became the sacrifice

---

242   1 Corinthians 6:19
243   John 14:16-18

for our sin and the sin of the whole world. Jesus bridged the gap between sinful humanity and holy God. Through Christ's Cross, the Brazen Altar is both fulfilled and rendered obsolete. No longer is there need for sacrificial worship. Jesus, the unblemished Lamb of God, has taken away the sin of the world, once and for all.

Setup Team: Place hammers, nails, red note paper, pens and a small container of red water based paint, and a Crucifix at the base of the full sized wooden Cross.

OUTER COURT & BRAZEN ALTAR

The Leaders invites people to the full sized wooden Cross. There on red notepaper they can write their sins for which they are seeking God's forgiveness and/or people they have made a decision to forgive. The pieces of paper are then folded and nailed to the Cross. The Leader models this, while inviting others to do the same.

(Power Point)

Outer Court & Brazen Altar
We Enter to Worship God

- At the Brazen Altar lambs were sacrificed for peoples' sins
- At the Brazen Altar Jesus made Himself an offering for us
- At the Brazen Altar we offer ourselves to God

READER 2 – At the Brazen Altar lambs, goats and bulls were sacrificed for the people's sins. Life is in the blood.[244] The sacrificial blood offering was essential for atonement, but it was also used for anointing in the consecration or setting apart of the Levitical priesthood and in rites for cleansing and healing.

---

244   Leviticus 17:11

READER 4 – By God's amazing grace, our faith in Jesus Christ not only grants us the forgiveness of sin and new life, but also makes us members of the tribe Levi. As the Israelites moved through the wilderness, the Levites cared for the Tabernacle's set-up, takedown and maintenance. Some were consecrated as priests to minister in the Tabernacle's sacrificial worship.

In Peter's first letter, we read about our new identity in Christ: *"But you are a chosen people, a royal priesthood, a holy nation, God's special possession, that you may declare the praises of him who called you out of darkness into his wonderful light. Once you were not a people, but now you are the people of God; once you had not received mercy, but now you have received mercy."* [245]

READER 5 – The book of Leviticus gives instructions for the setting apart of a priest: *Moses slaughtered the ram and took some of its blood and put it on the lobe of Aaron's right ear, on the thumb of his right hand and the big toe of his right foot. Moses also brought Aaron's sons forward and put some blood on the lobe of their ears, on the thumbs of their right hands and on the big toes of their right feet. Then he splashed blood against the sides of the altar.* [246]

Using red water based paint the Leader anoints a volunteer from the congregation (usually children and youth are the first to volunteer) according to the biblical instructions. People are invited to come to the Brazen Altar to be anointed by members of a ministry team.

245   1 Peter 2:9-10
246   Leviticus 8:23-25

READER 6 – The author of Hebrews tells us that Jesus:… *after he had offered one sacrifice for sin forever, sat down on the right hand of God.*[247]

Paul, in his letter to the believers in Rome, writes: *"The death he died, he died to sin once for all; but the life he lives, he lives to God. In the same way, count yourselves dead to sin but alive to God in Christ Jesus."*[248]

Further on in the same letter Paul writes more words of encouragement: *"For the wages of sin is death, but the gift of God is eternal life in Jesus Christ our Lord."*[249]

READER 1 – The wooden Cross is the New Testament Brazen Altar where God's only Son was crucified – the Lamb of God – who shed His blood and died to pay our sin debt. Here you may write on red notepaper the sins you confess with repentance and for which you ask God's forgiveness. You may also write words of forgiveness toward others. The notes are nailed to the Cross. After our worship the notes will be burned in the parking lot as an outward and visible sign of God's forgiveness.

MUSIC – "GLORY BE TO JESUS" (Power Point: Lyrics)

READER 1 – At the Brazen Altar Jesus Christ was crucified once for all. He paid the debt for my sin, your sin, all humanity's sin. Here we present ourselves (body, soul and spirit; past, present and future) a living and holy sacrifice, acceptable to God.[250] It is at the Brazen Altar that we cry out:

---

247   Hebrews 10:12
248   Romans 6:10-11
249   Romans 6:23
250   Romans 12:1

(Power Point: Order of Worship)

LEADER – Lord have mercy upon us.

PEOPLE – Christ, have mercy upon us.

LEADER – Lord, have mercy upon us.[251]

Setup Team: Bring into the Tabernacle and place at the Brazen Altar: Offering Plates, a Processional Cross, a Crucifix, a Chalice and Cruet of wine.

READER 1 – At the Brazen Altar we also find:

(Power Point)

At the Brazen Altar

- **Offering Plates**
  Give ourselves to God
- **Processional Cross**
  New Covenant Brazen Altar
- **Crucifix**
  Jesus offering Himself once for all sin
- **Chalice**
  New Covenant Cup of Salvation
- **Cruet of Wine**
  Blood of the Lamb of God

---

251 **1979 Book of Common Prayer**, page 356

The Offering Plates representing the offering of ourselves to the ministry and mission of the Church.

The Processional Cross represents the New Covenant Brazen Altar. The Cross of Christ always goes before us. It is to the Cross of Christ that we bring every situation and circumstance in life, for there we find Victory.

The Crucifix depicts Jesus' offering of Himself.

The Crucifix is placed at the intersection of the beams of the full-sized Cross.

The Cruet holds wine or grape juice that fills the Chalice used in Holy Communion, which is the New Covenant cup of salvation. Paul shares with the church in Corinth the words Jesus spoke at the Last Supper: *In the same way, after supper he* (Jesus) *took the cup saying, "This cup is the new covenant in my blood; do this, whenever you drink it, in remembrance of me."* [252]

The Leader and assistants unroll red crepe-paper streamers and sprinkle red confetti from the Brazen Altar to the Laver.

---

252   1 Corinthians 11:25 (addition mine)

A PATTERN FOR WORSHIP

READER 2 – For the twelve Hebrew tribes and later the nation of Israel, the Tabernacle was the center of worship, first in the desert, and then in the Promised Land where the Temple replaced the wilderness Tabernacle.

READER 3 – The construction of the Tabernacle was not left to Moses' imagination. God gave detailed instructions for every aspect of the design, materials, furnishings, priest's garments, and worship. The lives of God's people depended upon their faithful obedience. Disobedience, even in the smallest detail, could result in expulsion from the community or death. The Tabernacle is a lesson in God's unquestionable authority and holiness, as well as His expectation for our obedience.

READER 4 – In the book of Hebrews we are told that Moses and the Israelites built the Tabernacle precisely as God instructed, for it was:… *a sanctuary that is a copy and shadow of what is in heaven.* This is why Moses was warned when he was about to build the Tabernacle: *"See to it that you make everything according to the pattern shown you on the mountain."* [253]

---

253   Hebrews 8:6

(Power Point)

EVERY ASPECT OF THE TABERNACLE
HAS MEANING

Gold – Deity
Silver – Redemption
Brass – Judgment
Blue – Heavenly Nature
Purple – Royalty
Scarlet – Sacrifice
Acacia Wood & Badger's Skin – Humility
Fine Linen – Righteousness
Oil – Hoy Spirit
Ram's Skin & Goat's Hair – Atonement

READER 6 – Every element of the Tabernacle has meaning:

Gold represents Deity
Silver stands for Redemption
Brass means Judgment
Blue indicates Heavenly Nature
Purple symbolizes Royalty
Scarlet signifies Sacrifice
Acacia Wood & Badger Skins denote Humility
Fine Linen represents Righteousness
Oil represents the Holy Spirit
Ram's Skins & Goat Hair mean Atonement

READER 1 – More than a dwelling place, the Tabernacle and all its components were part of an intricate sensory aid to illustrate God's relationship to His people. One aspect of this relationship was God's requirement for complete obedience. God said: *"Make this tabernacle and all its furnishings exactly like the pattern I will show you."* [254] Neither Moses nor the Israelites were to stray from God's blueprint.

READER 2 – Their obedience was not only to be reverent in matters of the Tabernacle's construction, but especially in the way they worshipped. Any irreverence or ritual uncleanness could result in harsh consequences.

For example, the anointing oil and incense for the Tabernacle were made from God's prescribed spice formulas and declared holy. Both incense and oil engage the senses: the fragrance of spices, the sight of rising smoke, and the touch of oil. They could only be used for Tabernacle purposes. Anyone else using the same formula would be cut off from Israel.[255] The special garments for the priests were also holy. If the priests did not wear the proper clothing when serving the Lord, death could be the result.[256]

READER 5 – The Tabernacle of Moses is God's ordained pattern of worship. It is a pattern that has formed Christian worship to this day, and is evident to varying degrees in the liturgies and architecture of Christian churches large and small worldwide.

The Tabernacle of meeting was where God was present with His people. It was where sacrifice, atonement, forgiveness, prayer, and communion took place in the transforming presence of God.

---

254 Exodus 25:9
255 Exodus 30:34-38
256 Exodus 28:2 & 43

Setup Team: Prepare to place the Baptismal Font, a Bible, Lavabo and towel, pitchers of water, bowls and small towels for foot washing, an Aspergillum [257] and Holy Water.

LAVER

The Baptismal Font is placed behind the Brazen Altar. A Bible is opened to the day's reading and laid on the Font. Holy Water is poured from a large Cruet into the Font's basin. The Lavabo and towels are placed on the Font. An Aspergillum and Holy Water Bucket are placed near the Font and filled with Holy Water for the blessing of the congregation.

(Power Point)

The Laver
We are washed in the Word of God

- *"You are already clean because of the Word I have spoken to you."*
- A place to study Holy Scripture
- A place to confess our sins
- A place to forgive those who have sinned against us

---

257   In place of an Aspergillum a small bucket of water and palm fronds may be used.

READER 6 – The Laver was where the priests washed themselves after sacrificing animals on the Brazen Altar. It is where we are washed in the living water of God's Word. Here we listen to the Word of God read from the Bible and expounded upon in the sermon. Both the Scripture readings and sermon invite us to be vulnerable to God who works in and through us as ambassadors of His kingdom.

READER 3 – At the Brazen Altar animals and later Jesus died to pay the debt of our sin. At the Laver we die to self: our flesh or carnal nature, the world's cultures, and the temptations and bondages of the devil. Here we are raised with Jesus Christ to new life as citizens of the Kingdom of Heaven.

READER 6 – This is a place of new beginnings. The sacrament of Holy Baptism, repentance and cleansing from sin, declaration of our forgiveness, and forgiving those who have wronged us take place here. Water is what our senses encounter at the Laver. Water is the outward and visible element that communicates the inward and spiritual truth of God's Word. We are washed in the water of His Word.

READER 1 – The Laver remains prominent in churches today. It has become the Baptismal Tank or Font. A Baptismal Font is often the first piece of furniture you encounter when entering a church. Liturgical churches often have small basins of Holy Water at each entrance for people to reaffirm their baptismal vows by dipping their fingers in the water and then making the sign of the Cross, which is a prayer in itself to be offered with reverence: "In the Name of the Father, and the Son, and the Holy Spirit." If you want to make the sign of the Cross, follow me. Using your predominant hand, touch your forehead as you pray "Father"; touch your heart as you pray the "Son"; and touch the left or right shoulder at the word "Holy"; and touch the other shoulder as you pray "Spirit" – head to heart, shoulder to shoulder.

All the readers make the sign of the Cross as an illustration of the way it is done.

READER 3 – John baptized Jesus in the Jordan River.[258] The Gospel of Mark tells us that Jesus instructed His disciples: *"Go into all the world and preach the gospel to all creation. Whoever believes and is baptized will be saved, but whoever does not believe will be condemned."* [259]

READER 2 – Jesus' final words to His disciples are known as the Great Commission. These words are also instructions to His followers today. Jesus says to us: *"All authority in heaven and on earth has been given to me. Therefore go and make disciples of all nations, baptizing them in the name of the Father and of the Son and of the Holy Spirit, and teaching them to obey everything I have commanded you. And surely I am with you always, to the end of the age."* [260]

READER 4 – In Paul's letter to the Ephesians, he uses a marriage metaphor emphasizing the groom's responsibility to his bride, which is a picture of Christ's relationship to

---

258   Matthew 3:12-16
259   Mark 16:15-16
260   Matthew 28:18-20

the Church. *Husbands, love your wives, just as Christ loved the church and gave himself up for her to make her holy, cleansing her by the washing with water through the word, and to present her to himself as a radiant church, without stain or wrinkle or any other blemish, but holy and blameless. In this same way, husbands ought to love their wives as their own bodies. He who loves his wife loves himself.*[261]

*MUSIC (suggestion) – "THY WORD" –
Songwriters: Amy Grant & Michael W. Smith
(Power Point: Lyrics)*

(Power Point: Order of Worship)

1ˢᵗ ASSISTANT – The Holy Gospel of our Lord Jesus Christ according to John.

PEOPLE – Glory to You, Lord Christ.

2ⁿᵈ ASSISTANT – (Reads – **John 1:1-14**)

1ˢᵗ ASSISTANT – The Gospel of the Lord.

PEOPLE – Praise to, You Lord Christ.

READER 5 – Paul tells us that:… *the word of God is alive and active. Sharper than any double-edged sword, it penetrates even to dividing soul and spirit, joints and marrow; it judges the thoughts and attitudes of the heart.*[262] In response

---

261   Ephesians 5:25-29
262   Hebrews 4:12

to God's Word, we kneel and humbly confess our sins to Almighty God.

(Power Point: Order of Worship)

LEADER & PEOPLE – The Confession of Sin
Most merciful God.
we confess that we have sinned against You
in thought, word, and deed,
by what we have done,
and by what we have left undone.
We have not loved You with our whole heart;
We have not loved our neighbors as ourselves.
We are truly sorry and we humbly repent.
For the sake of Your Son Jesus Christ,
Have mercy upon us and forgive us;
that we may delight in Your will,
and walk in Your ways,
to the glory of Your Name. Amen.[263]

READER 6 – The apostle John assures us: *If we confess our sins, He is faithful and righteous to forgive us our sins and cleanse us from all unrighteousness.*[264]
Listen to the words that assure us of God's forgiveness.

(Power Point: Order of Worship)

LEADER – "Almighty God have mercy upon you, forgive you all your sins through our Lord Jesus Christ, strengthen

---

263 **1979 Book of Common Prayer**, page 360
264 1 John 1:9

you in all goodness, and by the power of the Holy Spirit keep you in eternal life."

PEOPLE – Amen.[265]

READER 2 – At the Last Supper, Jesus washed the feet of his disciples. Peter objected. Jesus replied: *"If I do not wash you, you have no part with Me."*

Then Peter said: *"Lord, not my feet only, but also my hands and my head."*

But Jesus answered him: *"He who has bathed needs only to wash his feet, but is completely clean; and you are clean, but not all of you."* [266]

Setup Team: Chairs, several pitchers of water, basins, and stacks of towels are placed around the Baptismal Font.

The Leader invites a volunteer to have his feet washed. Because foot washing is so far removed from Western culture, hand washing is offered as an alternative. People are invited to have their feet or hands washed by members of the ministry team or to wash one another's feet or hands.

READER 4 — Water is the outward and visible sign of the Living Water of God's Word that cleanses us from sin. Jesus is the living Word of God become flesh among us. Over time God's living and written Word forms the character of a disciple within those who have surrendered their lives to Jesus Christ. Jesus promised the indwelling Holy Spirit to

---

265   **1979 Book of Common Prayer**, page 360
266   John 13:8-11

equip believers for ministry and mission in the priesthood of all believers.

READER 6 – In gratitude for the Word of God and forgiveness of our sins, we stand and reaffirm our faith by sharing together in reciting the Apostles' Creed.

(Power Point: Order of Worship)

LEADER & PEOPLE – The Apostles' Creed
I believe in God, the Father almighty,
    creator of heaven and earth.
I believe in Jesus Christ, his only Son, our Lord.
    He was conceived by the power of the Holy Spirit
      and born of the Virgin Mary.
    He suffered under Pontius Pilate,
      was crucified, died, and was buried.
    He descended to the dead.
    On the third day He rose again.
    He ascended into heaven,
      and is seated at the right hand of the Father.
    He will come again to judge the living and the dead.
I believe in the Holy Spirit,
    the holy catholic Church,
    the communion of saints,
    the forgiveness of sins,
    the resurrection of the body,
    and life everlasting. Amen.[267]

---

267 **1979 Book of Common Prayer**, page 96

READER 5 – At the Laver we find a **Cruet of Water, Lavabo**, and **Towel** used to wash the celebrant's hands before serving Holy Communion.

(Power Point)

At the Laver

- **Baptismal Fount**
  - We die with Christ to the world, the flesh and the devil, and are raised with Him to new life
- **Holy Bible**
  - Scriptures read and Good News proclaimed
- **Cruet of water and the Lavabo**
  - The washing of the Living Water for service
- **Holy Water Bucket and Aspergillum**
  - No longer sprinkled by the blood of the sacrificial lamb, but by the water of our baptismal covenant
- **Basin and Pitcher**
  - Foot or hand washing

The acolyte holds the Lavabo in one hand, and pours water from a Cruet over the Leader's hands, then offers a towel that is draped over the acolyte's wrist.

READER 6 - At the Laver, we also find the Holy Water Bucket and Aspergillum used to sprinkle worshippers with water that has been blessed as a reminder of their baptism and as a blessing. We are no longer sprinkled with the blood of the sacrificed lamb, but by the water of our baptismal covenant.

The Leader sprinkles the congregation with Holy Water using the Aspergillum.

HOLY PLACE

The Leader unrolls the red crepe-paper streamers and scatters red confetti from the Laver to the Holy Place.

READER 5 – Now let's enter the Tent of Meeting or the Tent of Testimony. The first section is the Holy Place where worshippers become shut-in to God. In the Holy Place, we find amazing things: the **Golden Lampstand** or Menorah, the **Table of Shewbread**, and the **Golden Altar** or **Altar of Incense**.

This is the place where God met and spoke with Moses. It is a place of reverent prayer. The words that mark our entrance to the Holy Place are:

(Power Point: Order of Worship)

LEADER – The Lord be with you.
PEOPLE – And also with you.
LEADER – Lift up your hearts.
PEOPLE – We lift them to the Lord.
LEADER – Let us give thanks to the Lord our God.
PEOPLE – It is right to give Him thanks and praise.
LEADER – It is right to glorify You, Father, and to give You thanks; for You alone are God, living and true, dwelling in light inaccessible from before time and forever.

Fountain of life and source of all goodness, You made all things and fill them with Your blessing; You created them to rejoice in the splendor of Your radiance.[268]

(Pause)

GOLDEN LAMPSTAND

Setup Team: Place the Golden Lampstand consisting of six Processional Torches and the Christ Candle on the left side of the Holy Place. Place a Cruet of Holy Oil at the base of the Golden Lampstand.

---

268   **1979 Book of Common Prayer**, pages 372-373

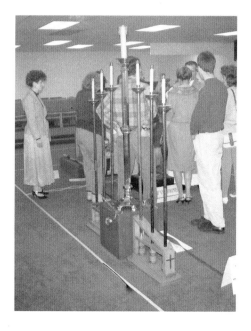

(Power Point)

HOLY PLACE

- **Golden Lampstand** or **Menorah**
  Declares the presence of God in the Holy Place
    - Oil representing the Holy Spirit for
      anointing, healing, and blessing
    - Light of Christ that pierces the darkness

READER 1 – The Golden Lampstand or Menorah was fueled by oil rather than wax. Light stimulates our visual sense. The Holy Place was constructed in a way that blocked natural light from the interior. Only light from the Golden Lampstand illuminated the Holy Place.

God gave Moses specific instructions for the High Priest: *Aaron and his sons are to keep the lamps burning before the Lord from evening till morning. This is to be a lasting ordinance among the Israelites for the generations to come.*[269]

READER 3 – The Golden Lampstand declares the presence of God in the Holy Place. God's light pierces the darkness of the fallen world. Our lives require not only natural light, but also the illumination of God's Light. Jesus says to us: *"You are the light of the world."* [270] Remember what you are!

READER 2 – The apostle Paul reinforced Jesus' words when he wrote encouragement to the church in Ephesus: *"For you were once darkness, but now you are light in the Lord. Live as children of the light."* [271]

READER 1 – The Golden Lampstand is made of six Processional Torches and the Easter or Christ Candle that proclaims the presence of our risen Lord.

READER 2 – One of the most powerful references to the Golden Lampstand is a warning found in the Book of Revelation: *"Remember therefore from where you have fallen, and repent and do the deeds you did at first; or else I am coming to you and will remove your lampstand out of its place – unless you repent."* [272]

---

269   Exodus 27:21
270   Matthew 5:15
271   Ephesians 5:8
272   Revelation 2:5

READER 6 – Jesus tells a parable of how ten virgins in a bridal party cared for their lamps. Five showed wisdom tending the wicks and keeping them full of oil. Five were foolish and unprepared when the groom arrived.[273] The point is that we are to be "ever-ready" with the light of the Holy Spirit for the coming of the Lord.

Setup Team: A Cruet of Anointing Oil is placed at the base of the Christ Candle. The acolyte lights all the candles of the Golden Lampstand.

READER 4 – Oil, in addition to fueling the Golden Lampstand, was used for anointing. God gave Moses an elaborate recipe for making a fragrant blend of Holy Oil. It was used to anoint things to be set apart as holy and to consecrate the Tabernacle priests.[274] Today Holy Oil is used at baptisms, confirmations, weddings and ordinations as a sign of the presence and power of the Holy Spirit. Holy Oil is also used to anoint the sick, the dying, and simply for blessing. It is an important part of prayer ministry for healing in body, soul, and spirit as the outward and visible sign of God's presence.

---

273   Matthew 25:1-11
274   Exodus 30:27-33

Oil Stocks are given to the ministry teams.
People needing prayer and/or blessing are invited to
receive prayer and anointing with Holy Oil.

TABLE OF SHEWBREAD

Setup Team: The Table of Shewbread is placed on the
right side of the Holy Place.

Have ready to place on the Table of Shewbread, the
Ciborium or Bread Box, Paten or plate & bread.

(Power Point)

Table of Shewbread
Represents the Bread of Life

- *"I am the bread of life, he who comes to Me shall*
  not hunger, and he who believes in Me shall never
  thirst." **John 6:35**
- **Ciborium**
  - Bread Box containing bread
- **Paten**
  - Plate to serve the bread

READER 5 – The significance of the table is in what it holds: the unleavened bread of God's Presence. God instructed Moses: *"And you shall set the shewbread on the table before Me always."* [275]

READER 1 – Moses had done all God instructed with regard to the table and bread. Boldly Moses addressed God: *"Now show me your glory."*

And the Lord said, "I will cause all my goodness to pass in front of you, and I will proclaim my name, the Lord, in your presence. I will have mercy on whom I will have mercy, and I will have compassion on whom I will have compassion." [276]

This is how the unleavened bread became sacred and known as Shewbread or the Bread of God's Presence.

READER 2 – The Bread of God's Presence in the Old Covenant has become the New Covenant Bread of Life. Our Lord Jesus Christ offered to us as we celebrate the Lord's Supper and partake of Holy Communion.

READER 6 – Jesus said: *"I am the bread of life, he who comes to Me shall not hunger, and he who believes in Me shall never thirst."*[277]

Paul writes that:*... when Jesus had given thanks, He broke the bread and said, "This is My body, which is given for you; do this in remembrance of Me."* [278]

---

275 Exodus 25:30 **New King James**
276 Exodus 33:18-19
277 John 6:35
278 1 Corinthians 112:24

We find a fitting invitation in the Psalms: *Taste and see that the Lord is good; blessed is the one who takes refuge in him.*[279] The bread engages our senses of touch, smell and taste.

READER 5 – Here at the Table of Shewbread that today is the Credence Table, we also find the **Ciborium** or Bread Box, unleavened **Bread** for Holy Communion, and the **Paten** or plate on which the bread is served.

The Ciborium or Bread Box and Paten or Bread Plate are placed on the Table of Shewbread.

MUSIC (suggestion) – "I AM THE BREAD OF LIFE" – Words and Music by Suzanne Toolan (Power Point: lyrics)

Setup Team: Have ready the lighted Thurible and Boat with Incense that are the working parts of the Golden Altar or Altar of Incense.

GOLDEN ALTAR/ALTAR OF INCENSE

Bring in a lighted Thurible and Boat with Incense and place on a fireproof stand representing the Golden Altar.

---

279   Psalm 34:8

(Power Point)

Altar of Incense or Golden Altar
The place of prayer and intercession

- The apostle John saw twenty-four elders
  "... holding golden bowls full of incense, which are the prayers of God's people."
- **Thurible**
  - Fire box of burning incense
- **Boat**
  - Container holding incense
- **Incense**
  - Our prayers of worship, thanksgiving, intercession and petition

---

READER 3 – The sight and fragrance of the cloud of incense smoke rising heavenward at the Golden Altar was visible evidence of the prayers of the people ascending to God.

Paul instructs his fellow Christians in Thessalonica to *"pray continually."* [280] This is a Christian's calling, to do as Jesus does for us. In his letter to the Romans, Paul assures believers that: *Christ Jesus is He who died, yes rather who was raised, who is at the right hand of God, who also intercedes for us.* [281] Jesus prays for us. We are to pray to Him for one another and the work of God's kingdom.

---

280 1 Thessalonians 5:16
281 Romans 8:34 **Revised Standard Version**

READER 2 – Malachi the prophet writes that the Lord declares: *My name will be great among the nations, from the rising to the setting of the sun. In every place incense and pure offerings will be brought to my name, because my name will be great among the nations.*[282]

The Book of Revelation pictures twenty-four elders falling down before the Lamb of God:... *holding golden bowls full of incense, which are the prayers of the saints.*[283]

READER 3 – At the Golden Altar we find a **Thurible** or firebox for burning incense, the **Boat** or container that holds the incense, and the **Incense.** Our prayers of confession, thanksgiving, petition, intercession and praise ascend before the Lord as a fragrant offering.

The Leader censes the congregation with the Thurible.

READER 6 – Let us pray together for the Church, the world, the needs that weigh upon our hearts, and our expressions of thanksgiving:

(Power Point: Order of Worship)

LEADER – Grant, Almighty God, that all who confess Your Name may be united in Your truth, live together in Your love, and reveal Your glory in all the world. *(A Minute of Silence)*
Lord, in Your mercy

PEOPLE – Hear our prayer.

282   Malachi 1:11
283   Revelation 5:8

LEADER – Guide the people of this land, and of all nations, in the ways of justice and peace; that we may honor one another and serve the common good. *(A Minute of Silence)*
Lord, in Your mercy

PEOPLE – Hear our prayer.

LEADER – Give us all a reverence for the earth as your own creation, that we may use its resources rightly in the service of others and to Your honor and glory. *(A Minute of Silence)*
Lord, in Your mercy

PEOPLE – Hear our prayer.

LEADER – Bless all whose lives are closely linked with ours, and grant that we may serve Christ in them, and love one another as He loves us. *(A Minute of Silence)*
Lord, in Your mercy

PEOPLE – Hear our prayer.

LEADER – Comfort and heal all those who suffer in body, mind, or spirit; give them courage and hope in their troubles, and bring them the joy of Your salvation. *(A Minute of Silence)*
Lord, in Your mercy

PEOPLE – Hear our prayer.

LEADER – We commend to Your mercy all who have died, that Your will for them may be fulfilled; and we pray that we may share with all Your saints in Your eternal kingdom.

(A Minute of Silence)

Lord, in Your mercy

PEOPLE – Hear our prayer.[284]

The Leader adds a concluding prayer. Cushions are placed around the Altar of Incense. People are invited to kneel and offer their prayers to the Lord.

WHAT THE HIGH PRIEST WORE

The Leader, already dressed in an Alb and Girdle, puts on a Chasuble and Stole. The Readers explain the origin and meaning of the High Priest's Vestments.

Setup Team: Have ready the Sanctus Bells.

READER 6 – When the priesthood was instituted in the wilderness, Moses consecrated his brother Aaron as the first High Priest of Israel. In Exodus, the High Priest's clothing represented his function as the mediator between God and the people. Today's Eucharistic Vestments are patterned after what the High Priest wore:

---

284   **1979 Book of Common Prayer**, pages 388 -389

(Power Point)

What the High Priest Wore

- **Ephod, a two-piece apron**
  - The High Priest was the mediator between God and the people
- **Golden Bells and Pomegranates**
  - Gifts and Fruit of the Holy Spirit alternated on the hem of the ephod to produce a pleasing sound
- **Breastplate of Judgment**
  - Representing the twelve tribes of Israel

Alb and Girdle – a long white tunic coming down to the ankles. It is usually girdled with a long white cord. Believers being baptized by immersion often wear these garments.

Stole – a sign of office that came to represent the yoke of Christ.

Ephod – a poncho styled garment worn when the High Priest entered the Holy of Holies once a year to make atonement for the sins of the people. Today the celebrant at the Lord's Supper may wear a chasuble, which is the equivalent of the High Priest's Ephod.

READER 4 – Golden bells and pomegranates were sewn alternately along the hem of the Ephod. The golden bells represent the gifts of the Holy Spirit and the pomegranates the fruit of the Holy Spirit. In the New Testament, Paul teaches that the gifts and fruit need to be in balance for the bells to make a pleasant sound. Otherwise they become like a clanging cymbal.[285] Our character is to be inviting, not abrasive.

READER 3 – The bells on the High Priest's Ephod rang while he ministered in the Holy of Holies, letting those who attended him know that he was still alive. Remember that if he was dressed or behaved improperly, he could die. Today **Sanctus Bells** have replaced the bells on the Ephod. They are rung at the blessing of the gifts of Bread and Cup during the celebration of the Lord's Supper.

The Leader places the Sanctus Bells in front of the Veil.

READER 5 – The High Priest also wore a breastplate of judgment set with twelve precious stones representing the twelve tribes of Israel. In the pocket of the breastplate, directly over the High Priest's heart, rested the **Urim** and **Thummim**. God communicated His will to the High Priest through the stones, which were like spiritual traffic lights: red for stop, green for go. God's Holy Spirit is our New Covenant guidance system.

---

285   1 Corinthians 13:1

OFFERING

Offering Plates are taken from the Brazen Altar and passed among the congregation.

READER 1 – Throughout the Tabernacle worship and our worship today, we continually offer ourselves to the Lord, remembering the words of the apostle Paul: *"I appeal to you, brethren, by the mercies of God, to present yourselves as a living sacrifice, holy and acceptable to God, which is your spiritual worship."* [286]

READER 2 – Let us with gladness present the offerings and oblations of our life and labor to the Lord.

OFFERTORY MUSIC — When the offering has been received and blessed by the Leader, it is placed beside the Golden Altar.

(Power Point: Praise Song Lyrics)

THE PILLAR OF CLOUD AND FIRE IS REVEALED

The Pillar is made of white, red, orange, and yellow crepe-paper streamers attached around the perimeter of a fan. The fan is behind the Holy of Holies, aimed up and turned on.

---

286 Romans 12:1 **Revised Standard Version**

READER 4 – Before going through the Veil and entering the Holy of Holies, we need to see what was above the Holy of Holies throughout the forty years in the wilderness. For the entire time of wilderness wandering, the Pillar of cloud by day and fire by night was the abiding and guiding presence of God.

READER 1 – The Israelites only broke camp and moved when the Pillar began to move. This means that the Israelites, particularly the Levites who were solely responsible for breaking-down, transporting, and setting-up all the elements of the Tabernacle, were very attentive to God's presence and movement.

READER 2 – In our exploration of the Tabernacle so far, we have examined the structure, materials, colors, and furnishings. The Pillar of cloud and fire is dramatically different because it was not put in place by the Israelites. We yearn to ask Moses, "What was it like meeting God in a bush that burned, but was not consumed? Tell me about meeting God twice on Mount Sinai? What was it like to follow the Pillar of cloud by day and fire by night all those years?

READER 3 – Moses' response could well be, "I had to climb a mountain to meet with God. What is it like to have God dwell within you every day? Tell me what it's like to have the Holy Spirit give you direction about where to go and what to say when you are clueless?" [287]

---

287   **not a fan.** By Kyle Idleman, page 91

READER 6 – The Pillar of cloud and fire prefigures Pentecost when tongues of fire separated and rested on Jesus' followers. Remember Jesus promised: *". . . you will receive power when the Holy Spirit comes on you; and you will be my witnesses in Jerusalem, and in all Judea and Samaria, and to the ends of the earth."* [288]

LEADER – If you have surrendered your heart to Jesus Christ and by faith accepted Him as your personal Savior and Lord, God's Holy Spirit dwells within you. You are a temple of the Holy Spirit. The apostle Paul assures us: *"Do you not know that your bodies are temples of the Holy Spirit, who is in you, whom you have received from God?"* [289]

Perhaps you are like me; there are times when I need to ask for more of God's Spirit. There have been times in my life when I did not pay much attention to the Holy Spirit dwelling in me. I have needed to ask God for forgiveness and yield my life again to the Holy Spirit. If you want to do this today, go to any of the ministry teams and ask for prayer.

---

288   Acts 1:8
289   1 Corinthians 6:19

VEIL
(Power Point)

Veil

Marked the division between the Holy Place
and the Holy of Holies

- Jesus said, *"I am the door; if anyone enters through Me, he shall be saved, and shall go in and find pasture."*
- Jesus opened the way for all believers to enter the Holy of Holies and into the presence of God.
- Jesus is our reconciliation with God, our way to God, our peace in God

---

READER 3 – The Veil marked the division between the Holy Place and the Holy of Holies. It was made of many layers of fabric and animal hides that could not easily be penetrated.

At the death of Jesus on the Cross, God tore the Veil of the Temple in Jerusalem in two from top to bottom. If a person dared attempt to rend the Veil, they would have tried to tear from bottom to top. No person tore the Veil; it was rent asunder by the hand of God.

The Leader draws back the Veil and
enters the Holy of Holies.

READER 4 – Jesus said: *"I am the door; if anyone enters through Me, he shall be saved, and shall go in and find pasture."* [290] Jesus opened the way for all believers to enter the Holy of Holies and dwell in the presence of the Father. Jesus is our reconciliation with God, our way to God, and our peace with God.

READER 5 – In most contemporary liturgical churches, the Veil is the rail or step to the Altar or Communion Table.

HOLY OF HOLIES

---

290   John 10:9

(Power Point)

Holy of Holies

The Place where we are in the Presence of God

- **The Ark of the Covenant**
  - God's Throne
  - God's presence with His people
- **Mercy Seat**
  - God spoke to Moses from the Mercy Seat
  - This is where God meets us

READER 6 – The Holy of Holies in the Tabernacle is everything from the Veil to the back of the Holy Place. In today's church the Holy of Holies is called the Sanctuary. Some congregations have moved the Communion Table or Altar to the center of the church.

The Holy of Holies was the place of communion with God. When we are filled with the Holy Spirit as Jesus promised, our spirit becomes the New Testament Holy of Holies. Remember to whom you belong.

(Power Point: Order of Worship)

LEADER – Jesus is here!

PEOPLE – Jesus is here! Alleluia!

LEADER – Lord have mercy upon us.

PEOPLE – Christ have mercy upon us.

LEADER – Lord have mercy upon us.[291]

READER 1 – The Holy of Holies was God's dwelling place among His people in the wilderness. Scripture tells us that: *In all the travels of the Israelites, whenever the cloud lifted from above the Tabernacle, they would set out; but if the cloud did not lift, they did not set out – until the day it lifted. So the cloud of the Lord was over the tabernacle by day, and fire was in the cloud by night, in the sight of all the Israelites during all their travels.*[292]

Setup Team: Place in the Holy of Holies — the Ark of the Covenant that contains the Paten and bread, a Bishop or Shepherd's Staff, and the Bible marked at the Ten Commandments. Exodus 20:1-17.

READER 2 – The Holy of Holies held only one piece of furniture: the Ark of the Covenant or Ark of Testimony, upon which the Mercy Seat rests, covered by the wings of Cherubim kneeling at either end of the Ark.

READERS 3 – Inside the Ark of the Covenant were two stone tablets containing the Ten Commandments,[293] Aaron's walking staff that continued to grow and blossom, and a pot of manna.[294] Through the fulfillment of Jesus Christ, today the Ark contains the written Word of God that is

---

291 **1979 Book of Common Prayer**, page 356
292 Exodus 40:36-38
293 Exodus 40:20 & Deuteronomy 31:24-26
294 Hebrews 9:4

the Bible, a bishop or shepherd's staff, and a container of blessed bread from the Lord's Supper.

(Power Point)

The Ark of the Covenant contained three things –

- Manna, the Bread of Heaven
- Aaron's Staff
- Unbroken stone tablets of the Ten Commandments

READER 1 – The High Priest entered the Holy of Holies once a year on the Day of Atonement, and sprinkled the Ark and Mercy Seat with blood from the sacrifice at the Brazen Altar.

The Leader, fully vested, unrolls the red crepe paper from the Golden Altar through the opened Veil and onto the Ark. Red confetti is sprinkled on the Ark and Mercy Seat.

READER 2 – The sprinkled blood signifies that the conditions of God's Law have been met: a life has been sacrificed; blood has been shed for the sins of the people.

READER 3 – God is just, He does not overlook sin. His Law is fulfilled by the obedience of His only Son whose sacrifice is mercy for all who believe in Him. The Ark proclaims that God, through Jesus Christ, is present among His people.

The Book of Hebrews tells us: *Therefore, brothers and sisters, since we have confidence to enter the Most Holy Place by the blood of Jesus, by a new and living way opened for us through the curtain, that is, his body, and since we have a great priest over the house of God, let us draw near to God with a sincere heart and with the full assurance that faith brings, having our hearts sprinkled to cleanse us from a guilty conscience and having our bodies washed with pure water. Let us hold unswervingly to the hope we profess, for he who promised is faithful.*[295]

READER 4 – The Ark formed the base of God's throne, which is the Mercy Seat. God is present with us in mercy. This was the most sacred and glorious object in the entire Tabernacle.

READER 5 – God spoke to Moses from between the wings of the Cherubim on the Mercy Seat. The Lamb of God, Jesus Christ, is enthroned upon the heart of every believer. This is the place of the treasured beliefs and memories of your soul. Your believing heart becomes the Holy of Holies. This is where Jesus meets you. He presses his heart against your heart.

READER 1 — Our journey through the Tabernacle has caused us to slow down and listen to the voice of God.

READER 2 — He is speaking to us and to His Church, welcoming us into His presence. Here we must stop and listen attentively. He is calling a priesthood to Himself.

---

295   Hebrews 10:19-23

READER 3 — All the baggage of religious trappings must be dropped at the torn Veil. You enter alone. This is not a place for credentials, titles, or gifts. Here we are terribly aware that we are humble earthen vessels. We stand only: *By the word of truth, by the power of God, by the armor of righteousness...."* [296] We recognize our own frailness. May the power of Christ rest upon you in this moment.

Pause for a moment to reflect.

READER 4 – Here we know as we are known in the unveiled presence of God. Here we are loved perfectly. This is what Paul called the more excellent way! [297] Here is the divine motivation behind every fruit of character, gift of ministry, call to mission. Within the Veil is God who loves you extravagantly.

READER 5 — In the Holy Place abide faith and hope; but in the Holy of Holies, the Most Holy Place, love abides. Faith and hope cause us to look forward. Love is a _now_ experience: His love shining into you — filling your heart with Himself.

LEADER – You have given your life to Him. You have surrendered your will to Him. The apostle Paul writes: *And God raised us up with Christ and seated us with him in the heavenly realms in Christ Jesus, in order that in the coming ages he might show us the incomparable riches of his grace, expressed in his kindness to us in Christ Jesus.* [298]

---

296   2 Corinthians 6:7
297   1 Corinthians 12:31
298   Ephesians 2:6-7

I invite you to be seated with Jesus on the Mercy Seat between the wings of the Cherubim.

The Leader invites two or three volunteers to sit on the Mercy Seat one at a time. Expect strong emotional responses.

READER 6 – You are seated with Christ Jesus in heavenly places. Paul in his letter to the Colossians assures us: *Since, then, you have been raised with Christ, set your hearts on things above, not earthly things. For you died and your life is now hidden with Christ in God. When Christ, who is your life, appears, then you also will appear with him in glory.*[299]

READER 5 – As you are seated on the Mercy Seat, determine that you will continue to yield to Him, to make Him your first love now and always. To Him you are totally committed. Your prayer is that His love will ultimately be the compelling force in your life, permeating your thoughts, words, actions, hopes, and dreams. His love has the power to bring you to your destiny and fulfill His purpose for the gift of life given you at birth and the new life given you at your confession of faith and baptism. Let's stand and proclaim the mystery of our faith...

299   Colossians 3:1-4

(Power Point: Order of Worship)

LEADER—Christ has died.

PEOPLE – We remember his death.

LEADER – Christ is risen.

PEOPLE – We proclaim His resurrection.

LEADER – Christ will come again.

PEOPLE – We await His coming in glory.

LEADER—By Jesus Christ, with Jesus Christ, and in Jesus Christ, in the unity of the Holy Spirit...

PEOPLE –... all honor and glory is Yours, Almighty Father, now and forever.

LEADER & PEOPLE – Amen.

READER 4 – The Tabernacle was built, especially the Ark, for God to be enthroned on the Mercy Seat where He was present with His people. The Ark is also called the Ark of Testimony, because of its contents. Inside the Ark are three objects, which tell the story of God and His people:

(Power Point)

The Ark of the Covenant

- **Manna, the Bread of Life**
  - Did not spoil in the Ark
  - God's provision to sustain the Israelites
  - Prophetic symbol of Jesus Christ
- **Aaron's Staff**
  - Jesus our High Priest to represent us
  - Jesus our gentle shepherd to lead us
- **Unbroken stone tablets of the Ten Commandments**
  - Jesus is God's unbroken covenant
  - Jesus is God's Living Word revealed in every book of the Bible

---

The Leader opens the Ark to reveal the Manna, Aaron's Staff, and the Bible as the unbroken stone tablets of the Ten Commandments.

LEADER – The golden pot of Manna that did not spoil and sustained the lives of the Israelites for forty years of wilderness wandering is now the Body of Christ, the Bread of Heaven in today's Holy Communion.

The Leader takes the Manna from the Ark and places it on the Table of Shewbread.

READER 3 – Aaron's Staff was so full of life that it budded. The High Priest's Staff speaks of our risen Lord Jesus who is our Good Shepherd. Today the Staff represents the Church's authority in ministry and mission to fulfill our Lord's Great Commission:... *go and make disciples of all nations, baptizing them in the name of the Father and of the Son and of the Holy Spirit, and teaching them to obey everything I have commanded you.*[300]

We place the Staff at the Tabernacle's Entrance to remind ourselves that we come and go in witness, ministry, and mission under our Lord's authority. He separates us. He calls us. He saves us. He anoints us. He sends us.

Aaron's Staff is placed at the Entrance/Exit to the Tabernacle.

READER 4 – Moses broke the first set of tablets in anger at the people's rebellion and idolatry. Humanity continually breaks God's Law. Paul writes a disturbing truth to the Christians in Rome:... *all have sinned, and come short of the glory of God.*[301]

The second set of tablets represents Jesus Christ, who did not break God's Law, for He was fully God and sinless man. Jesus fulfilled God's Law and set us free from its burden to live by God's unmerited favor. Jesus is God's unbroken covenant in the midst of a sinful people.

READER 3 – The Bible is the Word of God. Every book of the Bible reveals Jesus Christ to us. The author of **Psalm**

300 Matthew 28:18-20
301 Romans 3:23

119 proclaims: *Your word is a lamp for my feet, a light on my path.*[302]

The Bible is taken from the Ark of the Covenant and placed at the Entrance to the Tabernacle next to Aaron's Staff.

The Ten Commandments written on the unbroken tablets and all the additions made to the Law over the centuries by the Israelites, particularly the tribe of Levi, are fulfilled by the loving sacrifice of Jesus Christ. Jesus understood the enormity and burden of the Law to be summarized and lightened in a prayer prayed daily by the Temple priests: *"Love the Lord your God with all your heart and with all your soul and with all your mind." This is the first and greatest commandment. And the second is like it: "Love your neighbor as yourself." All the Law and the Prophets hang on these two commandments.*[303] We know this as the Summary of the Law.

READER 4 – In our worship we have come to the Ark of the Covenant, which in today's church is the Communion Table or Altar. Here in the Holy of Holies we will worship God by joining our voices with those of Angels, Archangels, and all the company of Heaven, remembering the words of Jesus at the Last Supper, and sharing the Bread of Heaven and Cup of Salvation.

(Power Point: Order of Worship)

---

302   Psalm 119:105
303   Matthew 22:36-40 also Mark 12:28b-33 & Luke 10:25-28

LEADER – Fountain of life and source of all goodness, You made all things and fill them with Your blessing; You created them to rejoice in the splendor of Your radiance.

Countless throngs of angels stand before You to serve You night and day; and beholding the glory of Your presence, they offer You unceasing praise. And so we join the saints and angels in proclaiming Your glory:

LEADER & PEOPLE – *(The Sanctus may be sung.)*
Holy, holy, holy Lord God of power and might,
heaven and earth are full of Your glory.
Hosanna in the highest.
Blessed is He who comes in the Name of the Lord.
Hosanna in the highest.[304]

MUSIC – PRAISE & WORSHIP (Power Point: Lyrics)

HOLY COMMUNION

The Chalice and Cruet of wine or grape juice are brought from the Brazen Altar; the bread is brought from the Table of Shewbread. All are placed on the Mercy Seat that has become the New Covenant Holy Table or Altar. The Leader fills the Chalice from the Cruet and offers prayers of institution and consecration from the Bible or denominational liturgy. At the consecration or blessing of the bread and cup, the Leader may invite people to join in the prayer by extending their hands toward the Ark.

---

304 **1979 Book of Common Prayer**, page 362

The following Prayer of Consecration is from the Book of Common Prayer.

LEADER – We give thanks to You, O God, for the goodness and love which You have made known to us in creation; in the calling of Israel to be Your people; in Your Word spoken through the prophets: and above all in the Word made flesh, Jesus, your Son. For in these last days You sent Him to be incarnate from the Virgin Mary, to be the Savior and Redeemer of the world. In Him, You have delivered us from evil, and made us worthy to stand before You. In Him, you have brought us out of error into truth, out of sin into righteousness, out of death into life.

On the night before He died for us, our Lord Jesus Christ took bread; and when He had given thanks to You, He broke it, and gave it to His disciples, and said, "Take, eat: This is My Body, which is given for you. Do this for the remembrance of Me."

After supper He took the cup of wine; and when He had given thanks, He gave it to them, and said, "Drink this, all of you: This is My Blood of the New Covenant, which is shed for you and for many for the forgiveness of sin. Whenever you drink it, do this for the remembrance of Me."

And we offer our sacrifice of praise and thanksgiving to You, O Lord of all; presenting to You, from Your creation, this bread and this wine.

We pray You, gracious God, to send Your Holy Spirit upon these gifts that they may be the Sacrament of the Body of Christ and his Blood of the New Covenant. Unite us to Your Son in His sacrifice that we may be acceptable through Him, being sanctified by the Holy Spirit. In the fullness of time, put all things in subjection under Your Christ, and bring us to that heavenly country where, with all Your saints, we may enter the everlasting heritage of Your sons and daughters; through Jesus Christ our Lord, the firstborn of all creation, the head of the Church, and the author of our salvation.[305]

(Power Point: Order of Worship)

LEADER & PEOPLE: By Him, and with Him, and in Him, in the unity of the Holy Spirit all honor and glory is Yours, Almighty Father, now and forever. AMEN[306]

LEADER: And now, as our Savior Christ has taught us, we are bold to pray –

LEADER & PEOPLE – The Lord's Prayer
Our Father, who art in heaven,
  hallowed be thy Name
  thy kingdom come
  thy will be done,
  on earth as it is in heaven.
Give us this day our daily bread.
And forgive us our trespasses,
  as we forgive those
  who trespass against us.
And lead us not into temptation,
  but deliver us from evil.

---

305 **1979 Book of Common Prayer**, pages 368-369
306 **1979 Book of Common Prayer**, page 369

For thine is the kingdom,
and the power, and the glory,
for ever and ever. Amen.[307]

BREAKING OF THE BREAD.

(Power Point: Order of Worship)

LEADER – Alleluia. Christ our Passover is sacrificed for us;

PEOPLE – Therefore let us keep the feast. Alleluia.

LEADER – The gifts of God for the People of God.[308]

READER 3 – In unity we remember what Jesus has done for us through His birth, life, death, and glorious resurrection. We remembered Jesus' Last Supper with His disciples. We have given thanks for the Holy Spirit's blessing of the bread and cup to become for us the presence of Jesus Christ. We have lifted our voices and prayed together the prayer Jesus taught His disciples. As the Bread is broken and the Cup offered, we are invited to again surrender our life to Jesus, and receive Him by taking part in the Lord's Supper.

READER 2 – Let us prepare to come to the Table of the Lord. Expect things to happen when you are in His presence.

---

307 **1979 Book of Common Prayer**, page 364
308 **1979 Book of Common Prayer**, page 364

Four members of the Setup Team offer Holy Communion at the Brazen Altar and the Table of Shewbread.

MUSIC FOR HOLY COMMUNION *(Power Point: Lyrics)*

(Power Point: Order of Worship)

LEADER & PEOPLE –
Eternal God, heavenly Father
You have graciously accepted us as living members
of Your Son our Savior Jesus Christ,
and You have fed us with spiritual food
in the Sacrament of his Body and Blood.
Send us now into the world in peace,
and grant us strength and courage
to love and serve You
with gladness and singleness of heart;
through Christ our Lord. Amen.[309]

MUSIC – HYMN - "CHRIST OUR PASSOVER:
(Power Point: Lyrics)

LEADER – (Blessing)

READER 3 – The Lord has promised to be with us always. Today God's Tabernacle, His dwelling place, is in the heart and spirit of everyone who receives Jesus Christ as Savior

---

309   **1979 Book of Common Prayer**, page 365

and Lord. We have seen that Moses' Tabernacle teaches the holiness of God and the sinfulness of man.

READER 2 – The Tabernacle mapped the way of salvation. Under the Old Covenant, salvation came through the sacrificed life and blood of animals, especially the life and blood of a sacrificed spotless lamb.

READER 1 – Life and atonement are in the blood of sacrifice. Under the New Covenant there is complete salvation through the blood of Jesus Christ. He is:... *the Lamb who was slain from the creation of the world.*[310]

READER 6 – No one else can save us. Salvation is not secured by works, but only through grace received by faith in Jesus Christ as Savior and Lord. The apostle John tells us: *The Word became flesh and made his dwelling among us.*[311]

Remember, the word "tabernacle" is the word for "dwelling" in the Old Testament. This means God came in living flesh to dwell or "tabernacle" among His people. As Jesus lived among the Israelites, He fulfilled the pattern of worship in the wilderness Tabernacle. The Tabernacle was the prophetic projection of God's plan for all creation's redemption. Today we are His tabernacle because He dwells in us.

READER 1 – It is difficult to leave this very special place and the experience of being in God's presence. We long to linger, remembering the words traditionally ascribed to David: *Better is one day in your courts than a thousand*

---

310   Revelation 13:8
311   John 1:14

elsewhere; I would rather be a doorkeeper in the house of my
God than dwell in the tents of the wicked.[312]
Before we go, there is more to see.

THE WAY OF SALVATION

READER 2 – As a portrait of Jesus, the Tabernacle points
to the Messiah, the Christ. Everything in the Tabernacle
foreshadows His Person and Work. Jesus proclaimed, *"I
am the way, the truth, and the life; no one comes to the Father, but through Me."* [313]

(Power Point)

JESUS CHRIST is the

- **Way** – *Outer Court*
- **Truth** – *Holy Place*
- **Life** – *Holy of Holies*

The **WAY** is represented in the Outer Court. Jesus is
the way from the outer court into the Holy of Holies.

The **TRUTH** is represented in the Holy Place by the
light of Christ, who is the light of the world. The Shewbread becomes the Body of Christ. The incense is both our
prayers and the prayers of Jesus who makes constant intercession for us.

---

312   Psalm 84:10
313   John 14:6

The **LIFE** is to be in the Holy of Holies. Because of the blood of Jesus shed for us, we can enter through the Veil, be in God's presence on the Mercy Seat face to face and not die. We have free access to God's amazing presence and the promise that we will be with Him eternally. *"God has given us eternal life, and this life is in his Son. Whoever has the Son has life; whoever does not have the Son of God does not have life."* [314]

A PICTURE OF YOU & ME

READER 3 — We've been looking at how the Tabernacle painted a portrait of Jesus, but it is also a snapshot of you and me. God is triune: Father, Son and Holy Spirit. We, too, are triune, created in His image and likeness.

(Power Point)

The TABERNACLE
A Portrait of Jesus
A Picture of You

- Our Body – Outer Court
- Our Soul – Holy Place
- Our Spirit – Holy of Holies

---

314   1 John 5:11-12

Our **BODY** communicates through our senses: the gates of touch, taste, smell, hearing, and sight. In the Tabernacle, our body is the Outer Court.

Our **SOUL** consists of our will, emotions, and intellect. In the Tabernacle, our soul is the Holy Place.

Our **SPIRIT** is comprised of our conscience, intuition, and capacity to be in communion with God, as we have just experienced. In the Tabernacle, our spirit is the Holy of Holies.

READER 4 – Our **HEART** is not only the pump in our chest that moves blood through our bodies, but spiritually, the place of the deepest thoughts and longings of our soul and the revelations of our spirit. In Ezekiel, God promises, *"I will give them an undivided heart and put a new spirit in them; I will remove from them their heart of stone and give them a heart of flesh. Then they will follow my decrees and be careful to keep my laws. They will be my people, and I will be their God."* [315]

READER 5 – One thing can deface the portrait of Jesus, the snapshot of you and me – **SIN**. Sin closes our ears to the life-giving Word of God. Paul warns us in Romans that, *"the wages of sin is death, but the gift of God is eternal life in Christ Jesus our Lord."* [316]

READER 6 – In Galatians, Paul encourages us to:... *walk by the Spirit, and you will not gratify the desires of the flesh. For the flesh desires what is contrary to the Spirit, and the Spirit what is contrary to the flesh. They are in conflict*

---

315   Ezekiel 11:19-20
316   Romans 6:23

with each other, so that you are not to do whatever you want. But if you are led by the Spirit, you are not under the law.[317]

Paul continues with assurance and strong encouragement: *But the fruit of the Spirit is love, joy, peace, forbearance, kindness, goodness, faithfulness, gentleness and self-control. Against such things there is no law. Those who belong to Christ Jesus have crucified the flesh with its passions and desires. Since we live by the Spirit, let us keep in step with the Spirit.*[318]

READER 1 – Our Christian roots are deeply established in the Jewish heritage. We have been called into God's presence and drawn to His heart. He assures us of our identity and destiny as joint heirs with Jesus Christ. We are transformed by His love, tender mercies, truth and grace to become new persons and embrace new life.

READER 2—God's redemption of the world is a process filled with events that began when Adam and Eve found themselves outside Eden's gate. The Old and New Testaments record the events of God's plan for redemption that culminates in His only Son, Jesus Christ. Church history is the record of our participation in the redemption process.

READER 3 – Likewise an individual's salvation is a lifelong process of sanctification filled with events, the most significant of which is our acceptance of Jesus Christ as our personal Savior and Lord. If you sense that accepting Jesus Christ or reaffirming your commitment to Him is

317   Galatians 5:16-18
318   Galatians 5:22-25

something you need to do, I invite you to the Cross. Many of these life events begin with God's invitation for us to draw closer to Him. Our acceptance of His invitation builds and nurtures godly character in us, equipping us as members of his royal priesthood to become effective in witness, ministry and mission.

READER 4 – We have seen that the Tabernacle is filled with invitations for each of us to draw closer to God. Come, come, come into the presence of the Lord.

READER 5 – Come, come, come and receive the blessings God has for you. Stay as long as you need. There are refreshments in the fellowship hall for your family and friends

When people have finished nailing notes to the Cross, at the Brazen Altar, I will remove them and take them outside to be burned. Our sins are forgiven and remembered no more. You are welcome to join me.

READER 2 – Come, come, come and be anointed and blessed. Wash the feet or hands of a family member or friend, or allow your own feet or hands to be washed. Come and sit on the Mercy Seat between the wings of the Cherubim. Don't leave with regret saying, "I wish I'd done that." You are welcome here!

READER 1 – From the last book of the Bible we hear these words that are an echo from God's promise to Moses: *And I heard a loud voice from the throne saying, "Look! God's dwelling place is now among the people, and he will dwell*

with them. They will be his people, and God himself will be with them and be their God." [319]

READER 6 – Like Peter on the Mount of Transfiguration, we are reluctant to leave this special place. We want to stay, to experience more. Our Lord has assured us that we are temples – tabernacles of His Holy Spirit. He promises to be always with us, even to the end of the age. We leave different than when we arrived. We've changed in ways that we may not yet be able to identify. This time spent at His feet will bear much fruit in your life. He has blessed you, and you will bless others in His Name.

(Power Point: Order of Worship)

LEADER – The Peace of the Lord be with you.

PEOPLE – And also with you.

LEADER – Please allow me to bless you with the blessing God gave to Moses for Aaron and his sons to use in blessing the Israelites:

The Lord bless you
and keep you;
the Lord make his face shine on you
and be gracious to you;
the Lord turn his face toward you
and give you peace. [320]

PEOPLE – Amen.

---

319   Revelation 21:3
320   Numbers 6:24-26

LEADER – Let us go forth walking by the power of the Holy Spirit, giving all the glory to Jesus.

PEOPLE – Thanks be to God. Alleluia!

In response to the numerous invitations made during the presentation, people have been exploring the Tabernacle in limited numbers. Now the entire Tabernacle is open for people to explore and experience the many opportunities to receive and give ministry. Members of the Presentation and Setup Teams remain on duty to provide assistance, prayer and ministry as needed.

In some traditions a pastor is understood to be an "icon" of Christ. As Christ's representative, the Leader may invite people to sit with him on the Mercy Seat and wait upon the Lord. The invitation and experience is valuable, whether people are alone or with the Leader. The option depends on the theology of the congregation making the presentation and an individual's personal choice.

The musicians are released to participate in the Tabernacle. The sound engineers provide quiet praise music in the background. Refreshments are available in the fellowship hall.

PART VII

JESUS STANDS AT THE DOOR AND KNOCKS

THE STORIES I'VE SHARED illustrate the importance of making invitations. They are only a small portion of the much larger witness of God's prompting to issue invitations and His responses to the needs of people at St. Mark's and Christ the King Church.

The scripts give a church community opportunities to practice issuing and responding to many different kinds of invitations found in Holy Scripture – invitations Jesus made and wants us, as His disciples, to make on His behalf.

My prayer is that both **The Gates** and **The Tabernacle** have and will continue to bless and even nudge you. What has been given to me, I entrust to you. You are free to use the scripts in full or in part, alter them, and give them to others.

In the **Book of Revelation**, Jesus makes an invitation that is a summary of all His invitations. He said, *"Here I am! I stand at the door and knock. If anyone hears my voice and opens the door, I will come in and eat with that person, and they with me."* [321] **Jesus is the invitation.** Jesus, who is the Son of Man, the only Son of God, and humanity's Messiah, yearns to enter your life. He stands at the door of your life knocking. He knocks in challenging circumstances,

---

321   Revelation 3:20

both bad and good. God loves you immeasurably, extravagantly, and unconditionally. He beckons you, "Come."

The invitation Jesus makes to you and how you respond is part of your story, as are the invitations you make to others under the guidance of the Holy Spirit. Those stories form your witness on His behalf; they also shape the ministry God has entrusted to you. The hard truth is that not everyone who is healed will come to faith and salvation. Likewise, not everyone who comes to faith will be healed. This reality should never silence our witness or halt our ministry of the Good News in Jesus Christ. Jesus made simple invitations. We can, too. Look to the Father. Listen to Jesus. Do what the Holy Spirit reveals to you.

Let us pray: *Father God, thank You for giving us Yourself in Your only Son, Jesus, and through Your indwelling Holy Spirit. With deep gratitude we thank You for the invitation You offer that leads us to faith in Jesus Christ our Savior and Lord. Form us to be like Jesus, making invitations with the guidance of the Holy Spirit. May Your transforming presence in worship help us become Your royal priesthood, a holy nation, equipped for ministry and mission in Your service. We are blessed by You to be a blessing. Thank You. All glory and honor to You. Amen.*

WA